CITADE
OF
WASTE

DAVID HILL

By the same author, in paperback and Kindle:

Their Greatest Disgrace - The campaign to clear the Chinook ZD576 pilots

(2016)

Breaking the Military Covenant - Who speaks for the dead?

(2018)

Red 5 - An investigation into the death of Flight Lieutenant Sean Cunningham

(2019, updated 2023)

The Inconvenient Truth - Chinook ZD576: Cause & Culpability

(2021)

A Noble Anger - The manslaughter of Corporal Jonathan Bayliss

(2022)

All titles published by Nemesis Books.

nemesisbooks@aol.com

The issues related in these books are ongoing, and they will be regularly updated. If you have purchased a previous edition, please contact the publisher for a free Kindle or pdf version.

All proceeds to St Richard's Hospice, Worcester

https://www.strichards.org.uk/raise-funds/

Contents

Author's notes

MoD is a Byzantine bureaucracy, impossible to fully understand. Readers who have worked there will appreciate that terminology changes daily, for no apparent reason. This book spans over 35 years, and to use the terms applicable at each event would be utterly confusing. In any case, I can't remember them. What matters is that I set out the problem, and show you how to prevent or fix it.

So, someone who manages a project is a project manager, not a delivery associate. I will refer to them as 'project managers' while recognising the significant difference between project officers, project managers and programme managers; and will differentiate only where necessary.

The dreaded acronyms... MoD publishes a 400+ page document containing the meaning of over 21,000 of them. (And it omits most of the important ones!) It's very existence reveals a huge problem. Watching anyone trying to decipher MoD papers and policies you can smell the despair, because they are written not only for a specific audience (which is fair enough), but to deliberately make it difficult for others. I can't say I'll avoid them, but I'll spell them out regularly.

I'm all too aware that many of the case studies might be seen as ancient history. But they are links in an unbroken chain, not isolated incidents, and I will demonstrate the core problems remain by joining the dots. And it is important to appreciate that the gestation period of major Defence projects can be decades. You should never dwell on the past, but you have to investigate and record it to learn from it.

The events herein are real, and fully documented. They describe and explain many failures. But also many accomplishments, and *they* show what can be achieved. Be of open mind.

Introduction

If you're reading this you're probably intrigued by the gleeful outpourings of the media over 'Defence procurement cock-ups', who simply regurgitate the words of Parliamentary Committees. The truth is usually very different; sometimes more complex, often far simpler.

Acquisition is *Requirements + Procurement + In Service Support + Disposal*. What the committees call *procurement* failures are often irretrievable fiascos long before procurers are involved. And I'll be offering many examples of successful *procurement* then undermined by poor *In Service Support*. Semantics? Not when some members take delight in calling for procurers to be sacked, knowing they have no right of reply. Their reports are a mixture of facts, ill-informed speculation, political points-scoring, and downright lies. Superficial, none even begin to look at root causes. (A factor that, if removed from the problem-fault sequence, would have prevented the undesirable outcome). We're fed stories of 'big-ticket' failures. A billion here, a few billion there. But they never mention the success stories.

Yes, there are certainly failures. In recent years perhaps the most well-known is Nimrod MRA4, scrapped in 2011 after wasting over £4Bn. But few realise, and MoD certainly won't admit, there are far worse examples. Individually they haven't all cost £4Bn. Cumulatively it's far more. And it's not always about the money. There's lost capability, and most importantly there are the wasted lives. What needs addressing is the impunity with which perpetrators act, and why MoD keeps putting them back into the system at higher levels.

Is it MoD policy to waste money?

It is an aspiration within MoD not to waste money. That is not in doubt. However, an aspiration only becomes policy when properly resourced. The resources required include clear directives and procedures - upon which much of this book is based. But one must be allowed to implement them, which has not been MoD policy or practice for over three decades. Every audit since 1988, conducted by both MoD (e.g. Equipment Accounting Centre, Director Internal Audit) and external bodies (e.g. National Audit Office, Public Accounts Committee), has found MoD wanting. Their recommendations were ignored.

What is the primary process for avoiding waste? **Requirement Scrutiny**, and conducting or contributing to it is an obligation placed on all staff by the Permanent Under-Secretary of State for Defence (PUS), MoD's Accounting Officer. That doesn't mean he's an accountant. He's accountable to Parliament, so answers before committees. And correct implementation of this obligation must be regularly verified.

Staff are taught that, when conducting scrutiny, one is not working for one's line manager but directly to PUS. Not *strictly* true, but it serves to emphasise the legal connotations. Those who sign requirements at the various stages have formal letters of delegation. They make a written declaration that scrutiny has been conducted in accordance with a set of rules. This applies to those who buy pencils or aircraft carriers. It is only the depth of scrutiny and level of approval that differ.

If one makes a false declaration, one is avoiding an obligation to PUS; which is maladministration and a form of fraud by misrepresentation. MoD does not consider this wrongdoing. I disagree, but concede MoD and Ministers have consistently upheld the ruling; so much so, MoD is permitted to commit extensive funding to upholding it. That being so, the inescapable conclusion is yes, it is MoD policy to waste money.

And before MoD disagrees with me, answer me this... *Why do you discipline staff who refuse to commit fraud and waste money? Well?*

What is 'waste'? Government defines it as:

> *Whether the cost could reasonably have been avoided or reduced by better judgment or management.*

This is often broken down into five categories: *overspent procurements, write-offs, contract cancellations, unplanned extensions,* and *administrative errors.* Correctly, *accidental damage* is omitted. A difficult area is *fruitless payments that cannot be avoided.* But there is one glaring omission:

Conscious waste

Politicians do not like to remotely consider such acts. Not least because they have been notified of them over decades and done nothing; and then watched while operational capability and effectiveness was degraded, and servicemen killed. This could have been *'reasonably avoided'.* When looked at this way, the wasted *money* is a sideshow.

The title I have chosen, 'Citadel of Waste', is a phrase commonly attributed to Gordon Brown when Chancellor of the Exchequer (1997-2007). He hung his hat on *'fiscal prudence'*, telling MoD to get its house in order. The trouble is, Chancellors are very busy, and implementation is delegated to junior Ministers. In this, Brown was poorly served.

I don't pretend these political matters are easy, or that *all* waste can be avoided. But I will show you what is possible, and how. I will address in detail alleged *overspent procurements*. I say 'alleged', because no political party or auditor ever mentions that a project may be overspent or over-budget (quite different things), but incur entirely *fair and reasonable* costs. If that is not acknowledged then one forfeits the right to complain.

My focus will be to differentiate between failures in the *Requirements*, *Procurement* and *In Service Support* phases. I will offer a broad selection of case studies and anecdotes, across many areas of Defence; although being an aircraft engineer many will be from that domain. Some may seem insignificant, but I will explain how they can, and did, mushroom and why most failures are linked, and recurring.

At any given time MoD has thousands working in project offices, each with similar tales. They know the big-tickets are *nothing* compared to the hidden truths; and through practical examples I will illustrate the everyday challenges they face, and what must be done to ensure the Defence equipment budget is spent wisely and efficiently. In doing so, I will always ask: *Why? Who benefits? What else is going on?*

For the purposes of this book the last is important. I want to convey that I am not looking at matters with 20/20 hindsight. If I discuss waste or a cock-up, I will offer a contemporaneous example of a similar situation that had the potential to be wasteful or a failure, and why it wasn't.

On a number of occasions I've been asked by committees, MPs and Ministers: *If you could make one recommendation...?* I'm always consistent:

Don't fixate on the failures. The vast majority of projects are successful. Ask why.

I

THE CITADEL

Governance [1]

The basic Defence model in the UK is that Head Office 'directs', Service Commands 'generate', and Enabling Organisations 'facilitate' or 'deliver'. Here, we are primarily focussing on the Commands who generate the requirements that the procurers deliver. A brief summary of the main components of this model, as applied to acquisition...

Defence Council

Via powers of prerogative, the Council gives the Secretary of State the ability to administer and command the Armed Forces through the Service Boards; the Admiralty Board, the Army Board, and the Air Force Board, which meet annually.

In recent years the power of the Council has been most evident in its decision to quash the gross negligence findings against the Chinook ZD576 pilots (Mull of Kintyre, 1994). However, it is not proactive, so has yet to address similar miscarriages of justice, by the same people; such as Nimrod XV239 (Lake Ontario, 1995). That will require another public campaign.

Defence Board

Also chaired by the Secretary of State, the Board is responsible for strategic leadership of the Department, focusing on strategy and plans for generating military forces, including financial planning, performance against those plans, and risk. It is the highest committee in MoD, and is responsible for the 'Defence Vision', which is:

'To defend the United Kingdom and its interests, strengthen international peace and stability, and act as a force for good in the world'.

(Noting a 'vision' is not a policy).

The Board's core tasks are:

- To help define and articulate the department's strategic *direction*, and provide a clear vision and set of *values* for defence.

---

1 https://www.gov.uk/government/organisations/ministry-of-defence/about/our-governance

6

- To establish the main *priorities* and defence *capabilities* needed to achieve the strategy.
- To ensure defence priorities and tasks are *appropriately resourced*.
- To manage *corporate performance* and *resources* in-year to achieve the required *results*.

Defence Audit and Risk Assurance Committee

The Committee reviews and challenges the Department's approach to internal control, and provides independent advice both to the Defence Board and Permanent Secretary. Its main focus is to ensure internal controls and processes are designed effectively and are operating as they should.

The permanent members are non-executive directors, the committee chaired by one of the non-executive directors of the Defence Board; at time of writing, the Chief Executive Officer of Ineos Energy.

Executive Committee

The Committee supports the Defence Board, providing leadership and decision-making across Defence. It drives the annual Defence Plan, and identifies and responds to risks and issues.

Investment Approvals Committee

The Committee acts on behalf of the Defence Board as the senior body in MoD responsible for decisions on major investment proposals. It sets and enforces the policy and guidance for all investment and disinvestment decisions, including where decisions are delegated. It reports to the Defence Board through the Executive Committee, and advises Defence Ministers on courses of action. Importantly, it approves the highest value requirements.

And those at the bottom...

Today, procurers sit mainly within one of 12 'Enabling Organisations'; Defence Equipment & Support (DE&S), a bespoke trading entity, defined by Government as *'an arm's length body'* of MoD. I've met no-one who really understands this, but one change was said to allow DE&S the freedom to retain, reward and manage its staff. (Its predecessors could always do this). Its purpose is to equip and support the UK's Armed Forces for operations, and is responsible for the *safe* procurement and *through-life support* of a vast range of equipment. (As were its predecessors). It works closely with customers in the Military Commands as well as with Head Office, and is entirely reliant upon their output. (So too its predecessors). If either err, particularly Commands when setting out their requirements, then DE&S must be in a position, and willing, to challenge and/or do their jobs for them; or it too will fail. (As with its predecessors). So what's changed? Is DE&S change for the sake of change? Has MoD's procurement organisation evolved, or regressed?

Essentially, these are the questions the Defence and Public Accounts Committees continue to ask when complaining about 'procurement disasters' and waste; so it would appear they, at least, see no improvement. They haven't offered any views on this, so I'll offer mine in due course.

These much maligned procurement staff spend their working lives being pulled in every direction by the decisions of the committees. Yet, astonishingly, are not represented on any of them, despite the Chief Executive Officer of DE&S being senior to many of the members and carrying infinitely more responsibility.

What if a real howler of a policy or directive is issued? The committees are unlikely to have anyone who recognises the danger. That will only become apparent later at the very lowest level - the project manager, whose reaction might be *'this defies the laws of physics'*, or a more straight-forward *'bollix'*.

This lowly pleb, in the final act before letting a contract and committing the money, must formally declare that the technical content and cost is *'fair and reasonable'*. He is the *only* person who makes such a written declaration. Everyone else is seen to 'agree by committee', and so is not individually liable. Would it not be better for someone with that ultimate responsibility to be involved much earlier, to apply realism? If you can't see and understand what's happening on the shop floor, that's not oversight, it's navel gazing.

Money matters

Authority

The authorisation of all expenditure is dependent upon the existence of a 'requirement' approved by the appropriate authority on behalf of the Permanent Under-Secretary of State for Defence (PUS).

It is a basic principle of financial accountability that, whereas (e.g.) the Chief Executive Officer of DE&S is accountable for all procurement decisions and actions taken within his own organisation, PUS is ultimately responsible for justifying the requirements placed on the CEO's staff by the rest of the Department.[2] He exercises this duty via a chain of delegation; these staff ensuring the validity of all requirements, according to their individual delegation.

Financial concurrence and scrutiny

Financial authority is not delegated through the Financial and Secretariat chain. Their responsibilities are as *assistants* to the project manager, and *advisors* on financial matters and approvals.

It is a common misconception that these staff *approve* expenditure. Rather, they confirm that financial aspects are in order; and that there is sufficient funding, in the right place, at the right time. However, they do have a *scrutiny* function to ensure the original approval is still being interpreted correctly.

Financial commitment

Similarly, it is widely taught that only contracts branches may commit the Department to contract. This ignores that the Safety Management System *requires* engineering project managers to be able to commit MoD at short notice and of their own volition.

I use 'project manager', but the MoD Technical Agency, responsible for maintaining the build standard and safety and, uniquely, named in the contract, exercises this authority on a daily basis. One person can do

---

2 CEO/DE&S was formerly the Chief of Defence Materiel, the post created in April 2007 upon the formation of DE&S.

both jobs, but if done separately the Technical Agency, which differs in that it is a formal appointment, has primacy on safety.

Technical and Financial Approval

Technical and Financial Approval are not separate delegations. It can only be granted to an engineer. If the project manager is not, he must defer to a subordinate who will have more authority and responsibility. A recipe for conflict. To avoid this, in the mid-90s MoD took the wrong path, it becoming common practice to allow non-engineers to self-delegate Technical and Financial (and airworthiness) approval. A bureaucratic 'solution', avoiding the real issue. The funerals of servicemen killed by this policy are sad affairs, the truth concealed from their families.

To get to this point, where approval is granted, may have taken years of work. Many valuable resources will have been expended, and funding ear-marked, only for the lowly engineer to reject the requirement. The way to avoid this is for the correct people to conduct scrutiny at every stage, and regularly verify it.

The decision to delegate is determined by a number of factors. From the early-90s the following were expressly excluded:

- Trustworthiness and diligence.
- Proven ability to make 'good' decisions, and a preparedness to back them up.
- Willingness to accept responsibility.

While it might reasonably be thought that the higher the grade the higher the signing powers, this does not follow. In practical terms it is the milestone values. If the lowest is, say, £10M, there's no point granting the project manager £5M delegation. If he's deemed competent enough to sign-off on the safety of the equipment, and take responsibility for the lives of those using it, then corresponding financial delegation should follow.

People are not resources, they are resourceful

Someone who is *accountable* is required and expected to justify actions or decisions to a person or body with greater authority, from whom the accountability has been formally assigned. Whereas, someone who is *responsible* has some control over or care for an action, or the obligation to do something as part of a wider job role, and is responsible to an accountable person. Both <u>must</u> be given authority commensurate with their remit. If not, then they cannot be held responsible or accountable.

The Defence Lines of Development (DLOD)

Eight DLODs underpin every requirement:

- Concepts & Doctrine
- Organisation
- Personnel
- Infrastructure
- Training
- Information
- Equipment
- Logistics

(I have included an Annex at the rear providing definitions).

These provide a mechanism for coordinating the <u>parallel</u> development of the aspects that need to be brought together to create a real military capability, which is the ability to carry out a task. MoD puts it well:

'Military capability is not simply a piece of equipment such as a tank. Rather, it is a tank with a trained crew that: can communicate with others on the battlefield; can meet identified threats; and can be properly maintained and repaired during its lifetime'.

Hence, MoD's 'Centre' in Main Building has Directorates of Equipment *Capability* (DEC) who are responsible for delivering it.

DLODs have always been necessary, only the name has changed. When they were announced in 1998 (initially there were six) many thought it a new initiative. In fact, the work had lapsed a decade earlier, but this was too embarrassing to admit. The trouble is, a decade is three or four generations of Service and civilian postings. The elements were correct but the corporate knowledge of *how to do it* was long gone.

The Senior Responsible Owner (SRO)

SROs are senior officers or civil servants. Incumbents are accountable to a more senior officer/official, and he to the Accounting Officer (PUS) and Responsible Minister. Their role is defined in guidance from the Infrastructure and Projects Authority as the person who is:

'Accountable for a programme or project meeting its objectives, delivering the projected outcomes, and realising the required benefits within the policies set by ministers. The SRO is the owner of the Business Case and accountable for all aspects of governance'.

He establishes and chairs the Project Board, and ensures there is the right representation throughout the life cycle. He seeks assurance that the project, including risk management, control, and governance issues, is being managed in an appropriate and effective manner. So, he's both *responsible* and *accountable*, but does he have the necessary authority?

The SRO's work is dominated by the DLODs. His Programme Team ensures that, if necessary, components which are prerequisites to the main requirement themselves become acquisition projects. These are the pillars upon which projects stand. ('Programme Team' is slightly misleading. They are not procurers).

As owner of the Business Case he is confirming all DLODs are robust and will be sustained. But he doesn't control this as he is not the 'owner' of any of the Lines, and almost immediately others can (and usually will) scupper best laid plans; for example, by constant reorganisation and cutting manpower. One problem is that the Chief Executive Officer of Defence Equipment & Support (the main procurers) is directly accountable to the Public Accounts Committee. This cuts across and sits uncomfortably with the SRO's role, creating confusion as to who is really responsible for what.

Importantly, the SRO's organisation must initiate the Risk Register, and the procurers inherit it. In real life this is rare. Allied to this is the mandate that, if it is known a risk will manifest, it is a *certainty* and must be mitigated before proceeding. The procurers can seldom do this and still maintain progress, as the aim is to stabilise key programme elements to provide a solid foundation.

It could be said fairly, then, that the SRO's real primary role is identifying and eliminating certainties. The golden rule is:

Avoid the avoidable, manage the unavoidable

Failure to do so lies behind some of the worst examples of waste.

I admit difficulty with the SRO concept and its implementation. Take any aviation project. For over three decades a standing risk has been MoD's refusal to adequately fund the maintenance of airworthiness. Every aviation SRO knows this, but not one has the authority to overturn the policy. The process of *managing* the DLODs was never resurrected, fatally weakening them. Later, I discuss an *ongoing* case where all eight DLODs were allowed to break down entirely before procurers were even involved - the Military Flying Training System. Despite constant notifications to the SRO, there was no intervention. The system had rendered him impotent.

The Project Manager

The project manager's job is to make decisions within his remit, seek decisions outwith his remit, and deliver to time, cost and performance. He may be a serviceman or civilian, and once appointed and given the go ahead to proceed, relies entirely on the SRO's output. He must be continually assured the DLODs are intact. If the project plan says *'The SRO will provide...'*, and he doesn't, then the project manager has a major problem.

If his superiors (his Executive Board) cannot resolve this with the SRO, he must declare planning blight, freezing the project. But if he did this every time the Service didn't state their own requirements, or DLODs were missing, then there would be precious few viable projects. One solution is to expand the boundaries of his remit by giving him the authority to take over. I offer some examples of this later that resulted in unviable projects being stabilised. But this can be taken too far, and a common failure is to plough ahead knowing there are major, and often insurmountable, barriers/risks to overcome. Such a 'can do' attitude can be a distinct positive, but one must know where to draw the line. As such, there must be clear criteria for declaring blight, and the procurers' Executive Board must oversee the process.

One key area that ticks off *technical* project managers is the persistent reference to the 'project team'. There is a notion, and all new recruits are taught, that the project manager will be surrounded by a horde of other 'managers' - Risk, Safety, Contracts, Finance, Quality, Technical, etc. This is utter nonsense, and therein lies one of MoD's most controversial, divisive and discriminatory policies. A *technical* project manager must be able to do *every* job in the team, but this is not applied to *non-technical* staff or *direct entrants*. The skillset forms no part of performance appraisal reports, and no credit can be awarded.

A *non-technical* manager will usually require substantial intra- or extramural advice and assistance. That is, depending on the background of the project manager, the direct cost of managing a project can vary significantly; affecting the Lines of Development, which are naturally predicated on a certain level of competence and experience. Similarly, if a *technical* project manager leaves, what was a part-time job may now need a team. Half-day seminars and numbers are no substitute for years of hands-on experience and know-how.

Therefore, there can never be a level playing field when determining if one is suitably experienced, the criteria for a number of crucial delegations. Nowhere was this illustrated better than at a Career Guidance Panel on 5 October 1998, when MoD set a delta for Air Systems project management <u>inexperience</u>. Having managed (not merely worked on) 125 projects, across all disciplines, and in all phases of the Acquisition Cycle (Concept through to Disposal), was now deemed too inexperienced for anyone above the most junior grade in MoD's Procurement Executive to be considered for promotion. But this was only applied to technical staff who were not direct entrants. The policy stood when I retired some years later, but like most isn't implemented consistently.

Pondlife

The vast majority of projects are not big-tickets; and most of the staff who make the associated decisions on what to buy, from whom, and at what price, manage multiple smaller projects. While I worked on my share of big-ticket jobs, I much preferred the variety of the latter, across a number of technological domains, and on different platforms, simultaneously. There, and unlike their big-ticket colleagues, one must be granted significant delegation, responsibility and autonomy. Either way, each bring very different challenges.

Many avoid the big-tickets because they can be professionally unrewarding. One can spend a career on them and never see the fruits of your labour. Take two new recruits to MoD's procurement organisation. The one posted to a big-ticket may be assistant to the minutes secretary at meetings. He books conference rooms, arranges coffee, serves it, and types out the draft minutes. But his colleague, who is equally qualified, may be posted to a project that is upgrading a front line aircraft, ship or tank. He will learn about managing the development of cutting edge technologies, and solving unique problems. He doesn't write minutes - he learns to chair the meetings and hand out the actions.

Which type is preferable in each post? It's horses for courses. But which is more useful when it comes to advancement? The one who has been tested in a wide range of situations and problem solving, or the one whose practical experience doesn't yet surpass that of a first-year apprentice? Having said this, I should set out MoD's formal position, relayed to us on 18 January 2000:

> *The ability to take minutes is a higher competence than the ability to simultaneously manage multiple diverse aircraft and equipment projects, which is 'low quality' work.*

Please remember that piece of perverted wisdom. It explains much.

The Provisioning Authority

The Provisioning Authority sits within the Service HQ. His job is to put the detail in the requirements that emanate from DEC in Main Building. He <u>must</u> be an engineer, as he is permitted to use engineering judgment to override the Permanent Instructions governing his work.[3] On avionics, for example, in each Service HQ there will be one for each broad discipline: Radar & Sonics, Comms, Navigation, and Electronic Warfare & Intelligence; and all must be interchangeable.

Once the equipment is delivered, he is seen to 'own' it, responsible for its disposition, availability, reliability, maintainability, overseeing modification programmes, and is generally the Service's trouble-shooter. When front line look at 'HQ', they look at him.

The role is like a sweeper in a football team. He takes an overview, spots what is <u>not</u> being done, gathers and collates the necessary data, and distributes tasks to the right people. Very similar to a Risk Manager. All

---

3 DGA(N) 125/1/8, Permanent Long Term Costings Procedures, paragraph 13.

project teams also need a sweeper, which my old Assistant Director graphically termed his 'Rottweiler'. He was spot on, because if there is no Provisioning Authority what is <u>not</u> being done becomes apparent far too late, requiring the Rottweiler to take over and bang heads.

In (e.g.) the RN the Provisioning Authority posts formed a section in London called Materiel Provisioning and Support Policy (MPSP). MPSP himself was a Commander RN. All his HQ staff were recruited from its own workshops, where they had received the same level of training as RN engineers, and were additionally examined in Civil Aviation procedures. When these workshops were privatised, HQs lost this natural recruitment ground. I'll discuss this in more detail later, as it remains one of MoD's most wasteful and destructive policies. If you get rid of the best engineering training facility there is, don't complain about lack of suitably qualified and experienced staff.

Also sitting under MPSP were the Service Engineering Authorities. Mainly very experienced Senior NCOs, their primary role was to sponsor tasks such as fault investigations and the development of modifications. They were placed in positions of enormous trust, with some permanently stationed at major defence contractors. Without exception, all those I worked with were superb, at the very top of their profession. The critical distinction was that the Provisioning Authorities were the interface, and the glue, between Main Building, front line, procurers and industry; whereas the Engineering Authorities sat between MPSP and front line.

Lastly, MPSP had the Ranging and Scaling Group (RSG), which was somewhat of an oddity. Its civilian staff had to be engineers, but the posts were deemed 'Limited Opportunity'. This meant one could not be promoted out of RSG, but had to go sideways and achieve two satisfactory reports in a 'normal' engineering post before being allowed to apply for promotion.

But the Provisioning Authority posts were abandoned in 1988 as a result of the Hallifax Savings, designed to reduce Fleet Air Arm support costs by 33%. Unfortunate timing, as the Wall then came down and further cuts were ordered under Options for Change. Who was to play the major part in achieving this? The self-same Provisioning Authorities. I'm afraid Admiral Hallifax's team rather assumed their roles would remain, it being so obvious the work <u>had</u> to be done; but didn't actually say this. Henceforth, the RN's position was:

The posts have been cut, so we no longer have the responsibility to do the job. It is now for the project manager as the next person in the acquisition chain.

If everyone took this stance, perhaps someone would take notice. But they off-loaded it in the wrong direction. They should've gone *backwards* in the chain, to Main Building. After all, it was a problem of the RN's making, not the procurers. A major disconnect was created, the procurers now stating much of the Services' requirement, also dictating and managing major support aspects. The vast range of tasks undertaken by the Provisioning Authority was now fragmented and uncoordinated, and only done if someone in the project team happened to know how. With the passage of time this became less likely. To the procurer, the man who had to formally declare that the cost was *fair and reasonable*, and own this decision, the most fundamental issue was that Service requirements were no longer quantified.

But if you don't quantify, you can't cost.

It would amaze you (or perhaps not) how many cannot grasp this simple concept. You don't go into Tesco and say *I want some toilet rolls*. The assistant will just say *How many?* and you look like a prat. Yet in 1988 this became formal MoD policy.

Provisioning Authorities prepared (e.g. Admiralty) Board Submissions, the purpose of which was to obtain approval to procure equipment (i.e. begin production), and subsequently incur expense.[4] (A previous, separate approval having been given to proceed with development).

In today's terminology, these are best described as de-bloated Business Cases or Main Gate Submissions (terms that were touted as a new initiative, but as with DLODs merely resurrected old practice). I won't go into the detailed process as it has recently changed yet again by adopting the 'Government-wide system for the launch and development of projects'; moving from a 2-stage to 3-stage process. Suffice to say, today's 'Guide to developing the project business case' is 134 pages long, which very few in MoD will have the time or mental fortitude to read in full. Whereas the permanent instructions for preparing a Board Submission are less than one-and-a half pages. (And rather neatly that was the maximum permitted length). Follow the latter and many today will say *My goodness, that's a succinct and excellent Business*

---

4 DGA(N) 125/1/8, Permanent Long Term Costings Procedures, Section 4.

Case. Who needs more?

Crucially, a Board Submission <u>must</u> contain, as an attachment, the final quantified requirement; giving a clue as to who should prepare it. Thus, the project manager learns precisely who needs to get the kit, and when.

But with the task defaulting to unprepared and under-resourced project offices, who could not guarantee expertise, the Services lost control. Despite, or perhaps because of the 134-page guide, the standard of Business Cases to the committees has deteriorated, most being illusory and unable to withstand proper scrutiny or true cost analysis. Reluctant to admit this, the requirement drifts or becomes a wet finger guess in qualitative and quantitative terms. Luck plays a major part. Has the project manager done this before when more junior? Is he willing to argue the Service's case for them? Will anyone listen?!

The Provisioning Authority must understand all the components of provisioning and support, and the variables therein; such as Fit and Maintenance Policies, Reliability, Usage Rates, and Recovery Rates of equipment requiring repair. Out of which falls concepts such as training and manning. If there's a support problem (and In Service Support typically accounts for ~80% of the through-life costs), one or more of these components has broken down. Lacking engineering judgment the 'answer' will always be *buy more*. He is responsible for maintaining the integrity of these components, and a key player in sustaining the Lines of Development. But then came the Hallifax Savings...

In the RN, the remaining staff transferred to the newly formed Aircraft Support Executive (Navy). There, their terms of reference were changed from 'managing' to 'monitoring'. The last time these former Provisioning Authorities had been monitors was on primary school milk duty. The new party line was: *Yes, we've monitored the situation, and know front line are in dire straits*, but staff were instructed to do nothing about it. Disheartened, most shipped out, leaving the remaining minor tasks to the Limited Opportunity postholders; who simply carried on doing Ranging & Scaling but little else. The posts went from being the best the RN could offer, to an unattractive professional backwater.

When the 'Limited Opportunity' policy was ditched the next generation of promotees was inexperienced and untrained; and their replacements had no-one to learn from. Front line still thought all they had to do was report a problem to their own HQ and it would be solved. Overnight, they found themselves completely ignored. The entire system failed catastrophically. One problem begat another. Later, I describe how three fully fitted Sea Harrier squadrons quickly became half a squadron fitted with navigation kit, and then there was an accident. A minor problem suddenly became a major flight safety risk. It's a vicious, vicious circle. And was happening across MoD, not just Service HQs.

The best way to convey this is to relate a discussion I had with an Integrated Project Team Leader, a senior RN Captain, when standing up his new team. He explained to his 90-odd staff what everyone was to do. Fine. But when asked who would make materiel and financial provision, prepare Board Submissions, act as trouble-shooter, and all the other Provisioning Authority tasks, he completely toppled. *That's got to be Main Building*. But *their* staff, sitting at the back as 'stakeholders', said, *Not us shipmate, that's a civvy job you've taken over along with the Engineering Authorities. Didn't you know they had the same boss?* A crack that had formed over a decade before had become a yawning chasm.

Now, compare what the Provisioning Authority is required to do, and the responsibility he has, with the minute-taker who is one grade higher. This inequity is a significant barrier to MoD achieving its acquisition goals. If you're a new recruit, needing good reports to advance, why would you take a job with huge responsibility and pressure, requiring 10 years prior experience, when a much easier and higher paid one is available, with no responsibility and no experience required?

So, while I will tend to discuss Provisioning Authorities in the present tense, I'm referring to the role and always asking: *Who does it now?*

Requirements Managers

The resultant problems with underfunding, and buying the wrong thing, in the wrong quantity, at the wrong time, became overwhelming. In time the concept of Requirement Managers emerged, DEC officers embedded in project teams. But too much time had passed and there was no-one left to teach them what was actually a minor part of the old Provisioning Authority role. More HQ functions fell into the chasm.

If asked to deliver what they were required to, their answer was invariably *'That's your job'*, meaning the project manager. None ever appreciated the irony that the Service's *Requirements* Manager was insisting on the project manager stating the Service's *requirement*. Their own organisation had failed them, placing untrained staff in posts with no information to guide them. You only ever have to ask them one question. *Who quantifies the requirement?* If they can't answer, the project <u>will</u> have major problems unless the project manager can do it himself. Not their fault. Just a fact.

And so to a main theme of this book. If the Provisioning Authority's job isn't done, is it a Requirements failure, or a Procurement failure?

It's a Requirements failure. Quite definitely, without question, the role belongs to the Service. It's all about *their* requirement, and maintaining the integrity of the assumptions and policies underpinning it. If they don't, then a project office must have someone familiar with the role. Even then, they're playing catch-up. But when there's only four needed for the most complex domain - avionics - that is statistically unlikely.

One solution mooted by the Defence Committee is a permanent cadre of *Service procurement specialists*.[5] It didn't realise it was speaking about *requirements*, and a compensatory measure to replace defunct civilian posts. But serving or civilian, where to get them from? The committee didn't say. As I said, the recruitment grounds were gone. And do servicemen really join up to do this type of work? There is certainly no evidence to suggest they do it better, and to achieve such a transition would take at least a decade, and cost much more.

An important point to understand here is that DECs are no longer permitted to specify what they want in anything but the broadest terms. To do so is termed 'solutionising'. They can only say *We want a means of communicating with someone 300 metres away*. They're not even allowed to say they'd prefer a radio. The delay while procurers try to make sense of such vagueness can be significant; which of course is the intent, as it delays expenditure. It's certainly not an attempt at efficiency, and is equally frustrating to Main Building and procurers. I recall when a colleague, recently transferred from the Department of Transport, was invited to procure precisely this requirement for those lads in Hereford. At the time we had MoD credit cards for minor expenditure, and he walked across the road to Argos and bought two kiddies walkie-talkies.

---

5 House of Commons Defence Committee report 'The UK's Defence Procurement System - It is broke and it's time to fix it', 11 July 2023, paragraph 152.

He wasn't trying to make a point. They met the endorsed requirement. In fact, he'd gone above and beyond, because signal flags met it. The users laughed; but the following day Director Special Forces descended to whisper sweet nothings in his ear. *When we say communicate with each other, we mean robust, waterproof, works in extreme temperatures...* Fine, but you didn't say that. Both learned a lesson, costing MoD £43. Better value than any half-day seminar.

The little cascade

For any given project, the further one works down the list of DLODs, the more frequently the task defaults to the project manager. This has always been the case. But if the SRO can't deliver what he is required to, what chance has the project manager? One mitigation was Service HQs having a coordinator, and in the RN that was the aforementioned MPSP. He and his staff worked closely with Chief of Fleet Support (Coord) and Resources & Programmes (Navy) in Main Building, and their own Plans & Finance. If the project manager identified a shortcoming, he looked to MPSP's staff, not Main Building. That is, they were the link between 'the Centre' and the procurers. Then the link disappeared.

The practical effect of these changes and policies was, within a few short years, middle and senior management in MoD procurement was almost devoid of people who had actually <u>managed</u> in each phase of the Acquisition Cycle. The problem this creates is a significant drain on the project manager's time. Hitherto, the system more or less guaranteed his immediate superiors understood intuitively. But now? A one line briefing became *War and Peace*, desperately trying to find a form of words to get the risks across to someone who can't grasp the links between *'There's no Safety Case'*, *'It's not airworthy'*, and *'You can never use the aircraft'*. Nimrod, in a nutshell.

I don't suggest this 'old way' is the panacea. Nevertheless, one simple fact permeates the case studies herein. The successful ones knew how to do the Provisioning Authority role, the unsuccessful ones didn't.

21

The procurement model

There are many ways to skin this cat. The difficulty is that this area of MoD has undergone so many changes, most staff don't know whether they're full-bored or countersunk. It's better to accept that who does what has little to do with one's formal role or terms of reference, but with who is willing and able.

The greatest obstacle is abrogation. Many a project manager has had to take on the role of others, both Service and civilian, because they simply refused to do their job. That sounds chaotic, and it is! But there's no point bitching about it. One has to adapt and get on with it, because the committees, and your own Executive Board, will be hunting *you* down, not the person who can't or won't do their job.

Perhaps the most blatant example, to me at least, was an aircraft *programme* where the endorsement said the specialist simulator Directorate would deliver the Mission Trainer. I went along to their boss to check all was okay, and that he understood I was contractually liable to deliver it for aircrew training in Month 42. He told me he'd scaled it at one project manager and two project officers, but the Executive Board had refused him *any* staff. And in any case, he'd not been given any funding. *Sorry pal, I can't do it. It's a DIY job.*

What to do? First, a major risk had become a certainty, but contractual penalty causes meant declaring blight would be hugely expensive to MoD. The 2-Star Director General, who sat on the Executive Board, was formally notified as to the impact of the decision. He issued his ruling quickly. As MoD's policy was that whoever identifies or notifies a risk must then mitigate it, the task was simply added to my job description. He was blunt. *Finish what you start, or suffer detriment.* My point here is that this book is about managing risks and, especially, certainties. Can you see why people would be reluctant to notify them in the first place?

There are four basic models MoD has flitted between over the years; and variants thereof. Taking Air Systems as the exemplar...

1. The platform office manages their aircraft, with specialist offices providing the aircraft equipment.
2. The platform office procures equipment peculiar to that type, with

common or generic equipment bought by 'commodity' offices.

In both, the platform office is responsible for systems integration and installed performance, but lacks control over what it is given to integrate. The line between them is blurred and one will always be able to point to exceptions to the 'rule', and the confusion this causes.

3. An 'integrated' project team who think they're doing everything, but in fact like everyone else rely on core or central services. This can go four ways. They duplicate. They each think the other's doing it and deliver nothing. The provider reneges. Or they get lucky.

4. This starts off the same as 1 or 2, but the equipment office reneges leaving it all to the platform office, who have neither the manpower nor funding. In an odd way many prefer this, as you know where you stand. It works best on relatively low value projects, say under £50M (which are the majority), as finding the shortfall is a routine expectation of any project manager. (Linked to the above risk policy, because to mitigate you have to first find the resources).

In a way, it matters not which model emerges on a given project. Success or failure depends entirely on the people. It's always about the people.

A related concept is 'cradle to grave' management, whereby a single project manager manages equipment from Concept to Disposal. This used to be termed Integrated Logistics Support (ILS).[6] The project manager was responsible for all aspects of development, production, support, etc. for a range of similar equipment. The term wasn't a particularly accurate description of the work content, but that barely mattered.

However, along came Defence Standard 00-60, entitled 'Integrated Logistic Support', and then it did matter. There were minor changes to the support aspect, but what concerned staff most was the confusion the name clash caused. 'ILS Manager' now described both MoD's most experienced equipment project managers, and new recruits given a discrete support task. The former had to ask that 'ILS' be deleted from their personnel records, and find new jobs. Otherwise their careers effectively began again.

---

6 For example, the MoD(PE) Airborne Radar ILS Unit was D/LRA23.

Practical project management

This section is illustrated by interweaving policy with a case study involving acquisition of an avionics system for RN helicopters.

The Acquisition Cycle

In MoD the CADMID Cycle has six stages:

- Concept
- Assessment
- Demonstration
- Manufacture
- In Service
- Disposal

CADMID replaced the Downey Cycle:

- Concept Formulation
- Feasibility Study
- Project Definition
- Full Development
- Acceptance and Approval
- Production
- In Service
- Disposal

I recall the first time we were told about CADMID. Everyone asked: *'Where's Development'? 'Ah, we don't do that now, everything's Commercial Off-The-Shelf. They just demonstrate it to us'*. Half-day seminars, eh?

The Cycle can be 50 years or more. (The Puma helicopter has entered its sixth decade). In that period there have been governments of different colours, each with dozens of policy changes affecting the originally approved project plan. The Defence budget is dangerously susceptible to these machinations, and it is the role of very senior officers to act as the interface between Defence and Government (at committees), and persuade them of the need for stability. But with one eye on post-retirement appointments, it is rare for them to speak out when in post. And with the procurers not represented, it's easy to see how things go awry.

How you get from Concept to In Service is mostly invisible to the end user. They want to know why they haven't got the right kit, in the right quantity, at the right time. They ask why we have no trained pilots, when billions of pounds worth of aircraft are languishing in hangars. Or why, in mountainous terrain on the other side of the world, and needing to speak to the UK, they are given radios with a range of a few hundred yards. They want to know *who benefits*, because they don't.

In November 1994 a secure (i.e. encrypted) comms system for RN Sea Kings AEW Mk2 and HC Mk4 got its fifth project manager in almost five years. Not one day's progress had been made. There was no agreed specification, and the requirement had not been quantified in any way. Yet very precise funding, to the £, had been approved. Clearly, there had been no knowledgeable input. Deemed an impossible task, the new incumbent was asked by his Director to have a final look, and if nothing could be done, cancel. No comebacks.

What to do? The following will give you an idea of what wasn't asked at committee, and what a project manager is required to know:

- The aircraft would be flown off aircraft carriers. As space on Invincible Class carriers was at a premium, and minimising variety simplifies all aspects of support while easing the training burden, every RN requirement stipulated *onboard commonality*. That meant assessing Sea King HAS Mk6, Lynx HAS Mk8 and the imminent Merlin HM Mk1. They had the same basic radios, homers and secure intercom. This had to be the starting point. (Sea Harrier was in the original requirement, but deleted because it is more simplistic).

- The AEW job was a technical and contractual prerequisite to a major project, establishing priorities and timescales. It had to be an upgrade to the Mk6 system. The Mk4 had to be an upgrade to Lynx, as they had a different clear (non-secure) intercom. The designs had to be upgradeable as various new technologies were under development, such as next generation anti-jamming.

- Procurement strategy. Too often, Intellectual Property Rights (IPR) are ignored. Few realise that the Provisioning Authority sorts this out

25

as one of the first tasks. He applies for an Airborne Radio Installation (ARI) number, and henceforth that is how the equipment is identified in MoD. The heart of the system was the secure intercom, ARI 23331. Five digits beginning with '1' or '2' meant IPR rested with industry. (Whereas the primary radars in Sea King were 5955, 5980 and 5991, and in Lynx 5979, the '5' indicating MoD ownership). The intercom was proprietary to GEC-Marconi Secure Systems in Basildon, so any other bidder would <u>have</u> to sub-contract them. Poor understanding of this is a major reason for project delays and fruitless payments, and was a large factor here. A dual-prime procurement strategy was developed; single tender GEC-Marconi for the avionics, Westland for the aircraft installation design, testing and trials. Such a strategy transfers some risk to MoD, so the project manager's background and retention becomes crucial. Because of this the project automatically attracted the attention of the Public Accounts Committee, and the SRO required weekly updates.

- Quantities. The SRO, Director of Operational Requirements (Sea) (now DEC), was unable to bring influence to bear on his own Service who, lacking a Provisioning Authority, had withdrawn. He asked the project manager to present his proposals. The most significant arose from a recent decision to cut the Sea King Mk5 to Mk6, and Lynx Mk3 to Mk8, conversion programmes. The surplus kit should be located and quarantined. The SRO promptly appointed him RN Provisioning Authority. He quantified the requirement, but to be on the safe side went high. It's difficult to put a figure on his 'error'; perhaps a million, but minor considering the £30M saved through identifying the surplus. Net £29M was good for a first day's work. But still some way to go.

Having made these decisions (i.e. followed mandates), the project manager could now sit down with GEC's Chief Designer and prepare schematics and Boundary & Interface Control drawings; and from them draw up an amendment to Appendix A to the Aircraft Specifications, listing the equipment to be fitted.

But a known standing risk remained. As a matter of policy the build standard of the existing equipment had not been maintained since June 1991, when the rundown of airworthiness commenced. (Exacerbated by the Home Office upgrading a technical specification which MoD had to comply with, but with no funding). This is <u>never</u> addressed in project approvals. Within 48 hours GEC were placed under a 4-phase risk reduction contract, the output to be a stable build standard, valid Safety Argument, and five production standard sets for the AEW Mk2. How can one scope and let such a contract so quickly? One *exploits* MoD's regulations, which I'll explain later.

The project was now well under way, and he set about writing the detailed specifications - agreed by Operational Requirements, GEC and Westland the following month. 18 months later the Chief of Defence Procurement was invited to approve <u>entering Development</u> just as the first <u>Production</u> equipment was being delivered. (Not that he was told this). The requirement was delivered under budget, and to a better specification than the RN could dream of. There. An example of what is possible, and common reasons for waste and delay.

What *should* have happened? Here's a brief overview of the process by which the Concept reaches the project manager as an endorsed Shopping List. For the most part I'll restrict myself to what is directly visible to him. Again, old terminology, but the principles remain...

'Requirements' are based on 'Assumptions':

- First Order Assumptions. The top level statement by government - *We will have a Navy, Army and Air Force, and they will do this...* In practice, and often for good reason, this is pretty vague.

- Second Order Assumptions. The Services' *interpretation* of the Firsts, breaking them down into (e.g.) types and numbers of ships and aircraft, their capability, and the Maintenance Policy to support them. (The Maintenance Policy must not be an after-thought. It is an up-front statement of policy. If it is wrong, so is all subsequent materiel and financial provisioning).

- Third Order Assumptions. The detailed Shopping List, prepared by the Provisioning Authority, sent to the Services' Resources & Programmes section, and thence the project manager, listing the precise numbers of equipment to be procured.

A Third Order Assumption <u>must</u> have an associated Second Order Assumption. If it doesn't, it's only a case of who cancels it first.

Self-evidently, this process had entirely broken down.

The overarching process (was) called the Long Term Costings, which is what is says. A 10-year look-ahead based on Assumptions, which change rapidly and often. Given this, the base data can never be truly up-to-date; so by definition the system *assumes* the costings cannot be accurate. The question is, by how much?

A lengthy period of bunfighting ensues, where requirements are prioritised, manipulated, and often butchered. This was called 'basket weaving', a perfect description whereby requirements were placed in virtual 'baskets', representing levels of priority and funding. A lower priority requirement could be 'weaved' into a higher basket if there were benefits in combining them - for example, technical prerequisites.

The key player is (was) the aforementioned MPSP, the Long Term Costings Coordinator. He and his staff must be wholly conversant with all three Orders; whereas Operational Requirements is primarily about Firsts and Seconds; and project managers can get away with just the Thirds so long as the others do their jobs. It can be seen why projects can succeed even if Main Building fail; but are at greater risk if there is no Provisioning Authority.

I've simplified the process, but I hope you are beginning to see that the procurers have little or nothing to do with building these foundations. It's all about the Provisioning Authorities, because it's *their* output which permits a sensible contract to be let; yet it's a constant struggle for them to deal with ever-changing Assumptions. It is here where the true cost of a project is established. The last real chance to avoid waste, but very often the first time knowledgeable input has been brought to bear.

Painting by numbers

This comms job was a technical and contractual prerequisite to the Sea King ASaC Mk7 programme. Had the correct number of aircraft (16) been endorsed to satisfy the First Order Assumption, it would have been Category A (over £400M), not B, and granted a significant team. Instead, it was 13 and the team comprised one full-time and two part-time engineers (one of whom was the *programme* manager, also managing the Sea King HC Mk4 avionics upgrade and most of the prerequisites). Yet 13 or 16 would have made no difference; all it meant was another three aircraft to convert under a different contract, managed by a different department. The key was to have the right *type* of people, able to make the right decisions.

The *programme* was given only 30% of the true cost, prompting some to claim it was in excess of £200M overspent. But with the *programme* manager again acting as Provisioning Authority, a *fair and reasonable* price was agreed for the Shopping List *he* produced.

Another example on the same aircraft... The Directorate of Military Communications Projects (MCP) was buying the Identification, Friend or Foe (IFF) equipment. The Fit Policy was 'Full Fleet Fit' (13), dictated by it being a safety and regulatory requirement. On top of this were Distributed Allowances - spares to support deployed aircraft, Typed Air Station, and populate the Integration Rigs. Also, the Post Design Services Sample Model, used to develop modifications and conduct fault investigations. Finally, Depot Stock and Contingency, plus a partial system for the Full Mission Trainer. The minimum requirement to support 13 aircraft was around 22, depending on reliability and how quickly they could be repaired.

How many did they buy? TEN!

How had this passed scrutiny? It must surely have crossed someone's mind the Fit Policy could not be met - quite important when the kit was mandated when operating in controlled airspace. No-one had spotted this. When asked *There's 13 aircraft, why didn't you challenge an endorsement for only 10?*, they offered blank looks.

The *programme* manager, not MCP, was told to do buy more, from existing resources. They cost £330k a pop. A ~£3M shortfall, plus through-life support costs. Not to mention fitting it to the aircraft and ensuring it worked. MCP said: *'If it works in the factory, it'll work in the aircraft'*. Sorry, if that's your level of thinking, best of luck with your 11-plus. But no problem, just shake the magic money tree.

The proper solution was for the RN to state the actual requirement, and run an Alternative Assumption (an amendment to the Main Assumptions). They refused. *Nothing to do with us, it's up to the aircraft project office to state the RN's equipment requirement, and find the money.*

This was recurring across all Air Systems. The *programme* manager was directed to slice something off the end of the RN's biggest ever, and perhaps most important, avionics programme. One slice was automatic target recognition software. Another, a new Electronic Support Measures system. (Telling you if you're being painted by a radar). On the aircraft itself there was pressure from Main Building to reduce the fleet to 10, it being left to the *programme* manager to make the case to retain 13. Only he pointed out and could explain why the actual requirement was 16, which is what won the argument.

He was allowed to buy a further four systems, meaning there was one spare. Who would be lucky enough to get it? At significant cost a role modification was developed whereby an older and less capable IFF could be slotted in when not deployed, to mitigate the legal aspect and provide some degree of safety during training, transit and delivery flights. One downside was the time and manpower needed to constantly swap equipment between aircraft. Less obviously, this degrades reliability, generating a requirement for even more.

This was summarised neatly by the aircraft office, to the RN:

'We would again highlight the recurring problem of the RN failing to make formal quantified Long Term Costings bids for avionic equipment programmes. To leave such decisions to the project office relies entirely on the project manager having an intimate knowledge of the Fleet Air Arm's past, current and future requirements. The information required to compile such a bid is classified and not available to us (and even then only someone with prior DGA(N) experience would know how to use it); therefore, any bid we make or advice we offer by definition includes more guesswork than should be necessary, in turn leading to greater errors in project funding'.[7]

The simple lesson here is: *If you don't ask, you don't get*. A significant number of 'procurement disasters' boil down to: *The customer didn't ask*. There was no audit trail to a customer requirement. The blindfolded procurer was pinning a tail on the proverbial donkey. But when the impact bit, the donkey kicked *him*. In fact, he was doing his best to get the Services *some* level of capability.

But the main concern, more than the financial shortfall, was that this IFF was a mandated safety requirement. Yet no-one except the *programme* manager and RN trials crews had shown the slightest concern. The entire process designed to avoid such failures had failed.

---

7 Loose Minute D/DHP 22/23/22/2, 22 May 1996, to DOR(Sea) RNA1.

Requirement Scrutiny

'The simple step of a courageous individual is not to take part in the lie'.
(Aleksandr Isayevich Solzhenitsyn)

Requirement Scrutiny ensures that, *from the customer's point of view*, and after consultation as necessary, *all* the considerations relevant to a case have been covered and exposed to balanced examination; and, if necessary, presented for higher consideration before any financial or contractual commitment is made. In short, this ensures the Permanent Under-Secretary's interests are safeguarded and that all requirements:

a) Have been correctly formulated, procedurally and in substance;

b) With regard to the programmed or *likely* availability of intramural resources, industrial capacity and money, and to current policy on (e.g.) competition, collaboration or sales, and;

c) Are defensible as proper, sensible and cost effective demands upon real resources and monies voted or *likely to be voted* by Parliament.

That is, b) and c) are based on *assumptions*. Therefore, before criticising any apparent failure, it must first be ascertained if the original assumptions remained valid. This information, including who negated the assumption, when, why, and what compensatory or corrective action was taken, will be available in the Project Diaries and Histories. Often the explanation is politically driven, with mitigation beyond the control of procurers; or indeed anyone in MoD.

These responsibilities must not be exercised in a passive manner.

Effective Scrutiny lessens the risk of funding being wasted. It must be carried out on every proposed expenditure, and be valid through-life. So, while Requirement Approval is granted at senior levels, the precise level depending on cost, the requirement must still be subjected to scrutiny at every stage thereafter. Fundamental here is that <u>approval does not commit money</u>. That decision is made by the procurer.

For the system to work effectively the original approving authority must not take umbrage at a subordinate later identifying an error; or, equally likely, a policy change undermining the original assumptions. Often the best approach is to accept that the decision was good on that day, but circumstances may change. Importantly, a good scrutineer doesn't just fail a requirement and walk away. If he cannot play an active part in at least suggesting mitigation, then he is part of the problem.

Opportunities for challenges are commonplace, but there is a reluctance to upset superiors. Staff might point out the original requirement *now* fails scrutiny, only to be told to sign anyway. That is, lie and commit fraud. Such orders are not illegal in MoD. Refusing to obey them is. The worst offenders are those who issue the orders, but do not have suitable signing powers themselves.

The above is key when considering the cause of alleged 'procurement disasters'. In the pages that follow I offer examples where staff inadvertently wasted money or other resources. To err is to be human. But I offer even more examples where staff made <u>deliberate</u> decisions to avoid their duty. *Do I obey an illegal order and commit fraud, or do I risk career-ending sanction by meeting my legal obligations?*

What matters most is this. A project manager will seldom have taken part in the initial scrutiny of what he must later Technically and Financially Approve, and procure. *Examples* I hear you ask... How about, an equipment buy approved for RAF Hercules that could only be used in helicopters fitted with Active Dipping Sonar? And the RAF refusing to budge when told. The basic error was failure to conduct scrutiny; but once notified the refusal to correct it made it a violation.

The biggest problem faced by procurers is the Service changing their requirement, especially after funding has been committed. In an unstable environment such as Defence this is often unavoidable. For example, the success of 'drones' (a term that has always had a completely different meaning in MoD) has forced a change in military thinking. The concepts of air superiority and battlefield management have been transformed. In fact, a significant part of Defence acquisition is working correctly if such changes *are* detected and nugatory expenditure identified. One must be able to react quickly to changing circumstances. This is, *avoid the avoidable, manage the unavoidable.*

For this reason an unavoidable change and subsequent cost increase cannot be categorised as 'waste'. It is a risk MoD takes, and a contingency factor is included to help cope. In this Defence is very different to most government departments, the nearest equivalent in recent years being the impact of COVID-19 on the National Health Service. It was totally unprepared, and the country urged to get out in the streets and clap those who dealt with it. But nobody claps when an MoD project manager is hit with a similar financial crisis through no fault of his own or MoD's, and quietly resolves it. He's more likely to suffer severe detriment.

Government employees and Crown Servants who cannot bring themselves to implement its policies are required to resign. Why do we not see mass departures? One reason is the waste described is mostly a consequence of MoD policy conflicting with higher government policy. (Although it is unclear which takes precedence). Also, types of policy may clash. Requirement Scrutiny is a financial policy, but disciplinary action for insisting on implementing it is an organisational/personnel policy. With different parts of MoD responsible, it is difficult to reach resolution without falling afoul of someone very senior. Often, staff just choose to avoid upsetting those who control their careers.

On the other hand, those who obey the law justify their actions by pointing to the legal obligations set out in their terms of employment. It is what prevents dismissal (but not threats of) because senior staff know it will be reversed at tribunal. However, this does not preclude reprisals; for example, denying promotion, unwarranted criticism, and so on. Again, and consistently, MoD has ruled this is not wrongdoing. I happen to disagree, but accept many do not, looking upon it as management tool.

Shortly before I retired, a young project manager in Bristol came to me for advice. He had been told to make a false declaration on a Command & Control System. He knew refusal to commit this fraud would kill his career. I reminded him of his legal obligations, which he knew very well. He protected his career. He'd moved to the dark side. Management had a new toy.

The 39 Steps

Responsibility for Requirement Scrutiny lies with Permanent Under-Secretary of State (PUS), and through him to Parliament and the taxpayer. Of course, one seldom engages with PUS (and he doesn't reply anyway). Nevertheless, when carrying out his bidding there are four fundamental questions to be addressed:

1. Is it a proper charge to Public Funds?
2. Is it affordable within budgetary constraints?
3. Is it a proper charge to Defence Votes?
4. Is it consistent with Government/Defence Policy?

One satisfies this duty by answering a number of detailed questions, and scruineers are provided with a list of 39, divided into seven groupings. The *39 Steps*, if you like, to avoiding waste. And the greater the cost, novelty or complexity, the deeper one must delve with each question. Formally, these are issued as 'Requirement Scrutiny Instructions' by the Assistant Under-Secretary (Finance and Secretariat). The version in use when I retired was dated 1 January 1988. It had remained current for decades as there was no need to change it. There also exists Joint Service Publication 414 ('Management Strategy') which requires Requirement Scrutiny to be conducted; but, as with most such publications, doesn't say how. They're written on the assumption that the Lines of Development, such as Training and Information, are intact. A fair assumption 30 years ago, but no longer.

I have structured Part II of the book around these groupings, offering a few examples in each. Not all are applicable to every requirement; but *Step 1* certainly is *('Why is it needed?')*. It must be answered with a summary of the background, including previous attempts to acquire the same capability. If this cannot be answered, the 'requirement' fails at the very first hurdle. Scrutiny is often *that* simple, taking seconds.

But very few scrutiny failures are complete showstoppers. The project manager is key (along with his risk manager if he has one, which is rare). Can he accept these failures, which he will view as risks, and still deliver to time, cost and performance? If so, they must be clearly articulated within the Risk Register along with the agreed mitigation; which should seek to avoid managing them through limitations of use and procedural controls. In fact, re-conducting (or revalidating) scrutiny is often the best starting point for risk assessments, as this will highlight most of the common programmatic, financial, resource and technical risks.

The catch here is that scrutiny failures <u>are</u> very often identified in seconds, but far too late. The obvious solution is to ask why this is possible, and by whom, and bring forward their involvement; raising a number of questions:

1. Who *can* answer these 39 questions?
2. Who is *told* to answer them?

3. Who actually *does*?

The answers are invariably quite different, a recipe for waste.

It will be obvious by now there is one key player who can answer most - the Provisioning Authority; and others can contribute. Therefore, who <u>coordinates</u> and has <u>oversight</u> of Requirement Scrutiny is crucial. Once again, and for good reason, the Provisioning Authority's boss is the Long Term Costings *Coordinator*.

While Requirement Scrutiny is a financial policy, there can be no reasonable expectation of a financier answering many of the *Steps*. So, while they issue the regulations, in practice they must leave it to engineers - and most gladly do. Those who don't... Well, I just mentioned Dipping Sonar kit approved for Hercules, it being important that the aircraft is stable in the hover. Not one RAF supply or finance officer who signed the requirement, up to Group Captain level, twigged that Hercules aren't. (Or perhaps they are. What do I know?).

All very amusing, unless you have the *final* signature and are of lower grade. In this case, the Group Captain attended a meeting on 30 May 1996 chaired by the Project Director, berating the decision to challenge.[8] All the while ignoring the Fleet Air Arm officers present, whose aircraft actually did hover. The Director (an historian and chemist) declared him barking mad. Which just meant a more senior RAF officer escalated the complaint. In the end it took the intervention of a Rear Admiral, declaring he would back the project manager to the hilt.

Requirement Approval should always be given in writing, as should refusals. And while it may be acceptable or unavoidable for an approval to be a few per cent out, I later discuss an Army requirement where the funding was less than <u>2%</u> of that required. TWO per cent!

The Approval must also state the amount of financial authority being given, and the limits of the tolerance which may not be exceeded without the case being referred back for further scrutiny. This used to be 20%, but was frequently compromised by Main Building not including VAT. Companies quote VAT-ex. A quirk of the system, which one needs to be wary of otherwise one's tolerance is immediately eaten up. Approvals are then copied to the procurers, and constitute authority

---

8 D/DHP/24/4/93/25 Minutes of meeting, 30 May 1996.

to begin the actual procurement process. The Service scrutineer must then ensure what is contracted conforms with the approval. Plainly, that must be the Provisioning Authority.

Now that you know these posts were effectively disbanded in 1988, does that explain a lot? Such as why project offices are routinely handed approved requirements that are impossible to deliver? Or aren't quantified and hence properly costed. Or duplicate a concurrent requirement, or a capability that is already in Service. These are just some of the issues I'll address shortly, offering and explaining the background to practical examples. But it will, I hope, be clear a solution exists. *Do what you're meant to be doing.*

A point of view

'From the customer's point of view' has always raised eyebrows, many believing this means the customer (the Service) has the final say in the requirement's approval. In practice it means the scrutineer must be able to look at what is proposed from the Service's viewpoint, but while heeding policy and being able to resolve conflicts.

These sound principles are compromised by MoD's personnel policy, whereby inappropriate self-delegation is permitted. This leads to situations where the senior person in a team may have little or no direct input to the decision-making process, with an engineer subordinate the *de facto* programme manager and team leader. In such cases it is better to view the senior as a 'team manager'; if indeed he is necessary at all.

Such an approach, albeit unofficial, has been successful on many complex *programmes*; one example being the aforementioned Sea King ASaC Mk7. But only until, in 2001, and 18 months before the In Service Date, the non-engineer was permitted to stand down his engineers, and set about overruling their engineering and design decisions to the point of rendering the aircraft unsafe. (The same official issued the edict on minute-takers, mentioned earlier). As a direct result, seven died in a mid-air collision on 22 March 2003.

That *programme* is today seen as a huge success; and in most ways it was, delivering a series of technical innovations years ahead of their time. But MoD cannot contemplate linking the illegal directives to the deaths, which are spun as a tragic accident. Yet the fact remains the main contributory factors identified by RN investigators were recorded as critical risks by the *programme* manager, but his mitigation work was cancelled. Not because the non-engineer thought them wrong - they were design and safety issues and he wouldn't know one way or the other - but because he *could*, with impunity. It was a narcissistic show of power, not management or leadership. He not only wasted money, but two aircraft and seven lives.[9]

What do the Services think of these non-technical civilians having the authority over the safety of servicemen, but no responsibility? I can tell you. They gape, incredulous at the project office junior making life-determining decisions; with his boss fluttering in the background making the coffee, barely able to take notes as he doesn't understand what's being said - yet permitted to overrule him without explanation or justification. Servicemen soon realise which civil servants they can trust. Industry is the same, with many companies keeping a 'little black book'. A couple of times I was allowed to see the Westland Helicopters one, kept in his bottom drawer by the head of Customer Services. It had a particularly revealing section on those who were deemed to have screwed the company. Top of his hit list was the Puma Navigation Upgrade, where Westland had stepped in and dragged both the prime contractor and MoD out of the mire, but received no credit. The ignorant dismiss them as *'Wastelands'*, but the list of projects where they've done this is long, and the waste avoided huge.

---

9 An investigation into the 2003 Sea King mid-air forms the bulk of 'Breaking the Military Covenant' (David Hill, 2018).

Boundaries

This section addresses what I believe is the main failure tending to undermine projects from the outset. Ineffective boundary definition and control, which is fundamental to the Defence Lines of Development (DLOD). This is established at project initiation, and determines the scope of the project and, crucially, makes clear what the <u>exclusions</u> are.

Traditionally, there are four basic levels in this process:

1. DEC, the Sponsor, and his Senior Responsible Owners.
2. The 'Steering Committee', the procurers' Executive Board.
3. The Project Director, usually the Assistant Director to...
4. The programme or project manager.

I want to discuss who or what is usually the weakest link.

Initially, DEC obtains approval for its requirement (e.g. from the Investment Approval Committee); confirming it passes the *39 Steps* test and that the DLODs are properly constructed and sustainable.

This is not just an approval, but an undertaking to the Executive Board, which gains its confidence via, mainly, the Boundary Control Document, and everyone on the control boundary agreeing to their role. It may not call it precisely this, but the auditable data must be there. The Board then undertakes to deliver to time, cost and performance, subject to the agreed boundaries and DLODs remaining intact. The standing caveat is: *If you don't meet your side of the agreement, or change anything, all bets are off.* All this takes place before the project manager is even appointed.

When debating 'procurement failures' <u>this</u> is where committees should look first. You will almost always find the root causes on the Control Boundary; and after that the failures cascade and multiply.

It is important to appreciate the dynamic that exists between these levels. DEC's themselves merely want a warm feeling; and in any case the Service culture teaches them to avoid detail like the plague. But is having a warm feeling, with no control, sufficient to expect them to take on the role of Senior Responsible Owner? What about the <u>actual</u>

responsible person?

On a day-to-day basis, project managers regard Wing Commander or Squadron Leader level as 'DEC'. The Services try to fill these posts with appropriate staff, but in aviation there is a tendency for them to be pilots. Engineering reality is applied much later, when regression is difficult without time and cost penalties. Either way, almost by definition these officers cannot have a procurement background, and are constantly frustrated by what they see as unnecessary bureaucracy. That is why they had Provisioning Authorities.

The Executive Board comprises 2-Stars and above. The only interaction I had with individual members was when they rejected my suggestions to make aircraft safe and not waste money. And they definitely didn't want to speak to me when the money was wasted and aircrew died.

The Project Director's job is to clear the path for the project manager, while staying out of his way. I was lucky to have superb individuals. In addition to major aircraft programmes, one had another minor task - the VVIP programme, to replace the Queen's Flight helicopters. I had to give him space: *'I've got Prince Andrew on my back. He won't tell me if he's speaking as a junior Naval officer, or as a junior member of the Royal Household'*. It was never clear to him who the Sponsor actually was.

When Kevin passed away, he wasn't replaced. The Chinook/Lynx Project Director was told to take it on; presumably in the early hours, as his evenings and week-ends were already taken up acting as front man on Mull of Kintyre. His main stressor was having to write letters to the families and legal authorities saying the aircraft was airworthy; and to the RAF and Ministers constantly reiterating why it was not.[10]

(Oh, you think I jest? The worst example I have documented evidence of is a critically ill project manager getting an e-mail while under intensive care, demanding he read some reports over the Xmas period and submit a briefing by end-December. His complaint was rejected).[11]

Boundary control is meant to be exercised via Service Level Agreements (SLA) between the project manager and stakeholders. This is well understood, and every project manager will have drafted SLAs. But very

---

10 The Mull of Kintyre case is the subject of two books by the author. 'Their Greatest Disgrace' (2016), and 'The Inconvenient Truth' (2021).
11 E-mail 23 December 2002 11:27 'DS2 SIRG'.

few will have received one back signed by a stakeholder, even though you're just reminding them what they're meant to be doing. The policy is not enforced by the Executive Board, so why be surprised if a project falters? In fact, the first SLA should always be with the Executive Board. Although when I tried this the silence was deafening. What got a reaction was then naming individual members in the Risk Register as Risk Owners. I was told in no uncertain terms that *procurement* risks were of *'no concern'* to the *procurement* Executive Board.

Notwithstanding my insolence, who is meant to oversee this? DEC has the responsibility, but not the authority. The head procurer (who is not a procurer) has the authority, but doesn't exercise it, is not held responsible, and allows his Executive Board to mark their own homework. If the project manager ever gets a response, it's *'DIY'*. Which is the default position anyway, as he must be able to do all jobs in the team - and the jobs of other teams. I never did understand what added value the Executive Board brought to the table.

Instead of a 'Requirements Manager' embedded in the project team, what is needed, at a minimum, is an experienced (but independent) Provisioning Authority and procurer embedded in each DEC, to bring engineering judgment and pragmatism to bear far earlier in the project. That is, conduct Requirement Scrutiny. But you'd have to pay them a lot more, because their salaries wouldn't fund a cardboard box under Charing Cross Bridge.

MoD retains superior technical staff, but the demographic is worrying. Any organisation that relies on retired staff re-joining - some via consultancy agencies, others on part-time contracts - is in dire straits. By definition, MoD has admitted these retirees are the last of a breed. That, the change in recruitment and manning policies of the 90s and 00s didn't work. Another indicator is the sheer volume of routine work that is now 'outsourced', at disproportionate cost. Is that where the Defence equipment budget should be spent? Correctly, these ex-MoD staff and agencies sit at an even greater distance from the key decision points; but when eventually unshackled are left to pick up even more fragmented pieces, because there is very little remaining corporate knowledge or experience. In 10 years, when they are in their late-70s, who's going to be left? Those who felt the need to engage them in the first place, because they couldn't do what they were meant to be doing themselves. That's what happens when you run MoD as a business.

'Savings' at the expense of safety

This rather acerbic and irreverent section presents evidence of RAF policy decisions notified to the Nimrod Review in 2007; set up after the loss of Nimrod XV230 in 2006, killing 14, and in which Mr Charles Haddon-Cave QC (now Sir Charles KC) confirmed:

'Business goals and achieving savings and efficiency targets became the paramount focus of their time and attention, at the expense of safety and airworthiness matters such as the Nimrod Safety Case'.

Mr Haddon-Cave dated this at 1998, claiming it arose from that year's Strategic Defence Review. He then contradicted himself by citing the 1996 Nimrod Airworthiness Review Team report; which had reiterated the failings noted in 1992 by the RAF Director of Flight Safety; in turn repeating notifications and warnings from project managers in 1988.

That said, his recommendations were excellent, although mostly mandated policy anyway (which he didn't mention). But this incorrect dating of the key event served to protect certain senior RAF officers. Knowing their names were all over the destructive policies and events of the previous two decades, Mr Haddon-Cave named and praised them; when the truth was laid bare in RAF correspondence and reports.

What few appreciate, because MoD and Government seek to compartmentalise, is the truth was brutally exposed two years later by Lord Philip in his Mull of Kintyre Review. Given precisely the same evidence, he confirmed the effects of the policies were evident in the early 90s. The Government accepted both reports, but on this central point only one was accurate.

Before, in the beginning

Leaflet DM87 to Air Publication 830 (the 'Supply Handbook') was being formulated as a policy throughout the first half of 1987, by Air Member Supply and Organisation (RAF) (AMSO). It was a significant Leaflet, some 30 pages plus Annexes, and went through many drafts.[12]

Those in MoD whom it would affect most, the Service HQs and procurers, were not told the policy was even being considered. The first

---

12 When discussing AMSO, I am referring to the Organisation, not AMSO himself.

the latter knew at a working level (Assistant Director and below), was the circulation of a new clause on 12 January 1988 to be inserted in repair contracts with immediate effect. This denied contractors access to a number of 'excluded ranges', including Section 10 (Electronic) spares. In many cases these had been bought for the sole use of said contractors. Overnight they were rendered surplus.

AMSO argued that industry *had* been advised, via a short piece next to an obituary in the 13 January 1988 issue of THESBAC, the circular of the Society of British Aerospace Companies. The two dates tell you everything. AMSO placed the onus on the Society to inform its members. Of what was unclear, because it had not circulated the actual policy or how it was to be implemented. In fact, AP830 was not readily available to anyone outside AMSO, even if they knew of it.

A directive was issued that all excluded range holdings at contractors were to be scrapped, and the companies should now buy the spares themselves. One problem was that many electronic components contain hazardous substances whose disposal must be carefully controlled, and is often expensive. AMSO demanded the companies pay for this themselves. Moreover, while RAF suppliers issued the policy, industry were told to take any complaints to unsuspecting project offices in MoD's Procurement Executive.

This could not be suddenly dropped on industry. Extant contracts guaranteed them access to MoD stores, so they had no need to enter into comprehensive arrangements with suppliers. Nor was there sufficient financial sanction on any contract to cover this new cost. The policy failed scrutiny, the immediate and obvious showstopper being the up-front costs which would be incurred. Even if approved, a minimum of three years would be required (the financial bidding process, plus production lead-times) before the change-over could commence. The project offices recommended that contractors be permitted to use up existing spares. Anything but scrap them. AMSO refused.

Any request for funding to implement and compensate for this waste would expose AMSO to ridicule, so they faced having to generate funding from within the existing budget. Because the Long Term Costings Instructions required the holding of Depot Stock, Contingency (16% of Depot Stock), and War Reserves, the effect was at first gradual. This kit was committed to purposes for which it was not intended, hiding the problem for a while, but the medium and long-term effect was ruinous. The immediate effects were:

- MoD was placed in contractual default for not supplying spares.
- Repair contracts had to be amended and funded to allow contractors to buy these replacements. Prohibited from buying economic quantities, unit prices increased.
- Extended repair times.
- Air Stations attempted repairs they were not capable of, often damaging the equipment even more and making it unsafe.

This farcical situation, whereby front line was desperate for kit, and contractors had the necessary spares to effect repairs but were under orders to scrap them, was compounded by suppliers raising requisitions to replace the scrapped spares. Which, when delivered, would promptly be scrapped. Which would generate another requisition... This continued for at least eight years, evidenced by a Director Internal Audit report of June 1996, discussed later.

It took some time to uncover who was involved, but in August 1988 the author of DM87, SS9B(RAF), was tracked down and engaged. This RAF officer, a Wing Commander in Empress State Building, London, confirmed interpretation and implementation of DM87 was incorrect. His superiors disagreed, insisting the waste continue.

The effect was rammed fully home to front line in March 1990. RAF Hercules were suffering cracked Cloud and Collision Warning Radar scanner gearboxes. If they broke-up in fight the debris could cause untold damage. Supply managers refused to release funding for the engineering investigation into this critical flight safety hazard. The RAF's Director of Flight Safety later called this the *'principal airworthiness hazard to the routine operation of the aircraft'*[13] The suppliers, the Assistant Chief of the Air Staff, and the RAF's Chief Engineer, ignored him. What, they asked, could the Director of Flight Safety know about... flight safety. And yet, the post is a personal appointment of the Chief of the Air Staff. When this occurs, something lies beneath which someone wants to remain hidden.

On this radar (also fitted to Jetstream, Dominie, VC10 and Andover), the annual waste exceeded £3M in the first year. It was one of hundreds of avionic equipments subject to the policy. Within three months of Financial Year 1988/89 commencing, a whole-year overspend on repair contracts loomed. Contracts were suspended or cancelled; repeated

---

13 D/IFS(RAF)/125/44/2/2. Hercules Airworthiness Review Team Report, paragraph 6.

again the following year.

In what way was DM87 thought to be a 'savings measure'? AMSO's position was they would no longer have to pay for the spares, storage and distribution; ignoring these costs would just be charged against the repair contract, and there would be an admin overhead. Most obviously, spares that had previously been bought in bulk would now have to be bought in smaller quantities by scores of companies, with none having access to the others' stock. The impact, equipment shortages and vast waste, was deemed irrelevant. The cynical (with some justification) thought it an attempt to get a promotion tick in the box; existing stocks hiding the problem until the current postholders moved on.

The absurd thing is, that with DM87 AMSO knowingly shot themselves well and truly in the foot. This was idiocy beyond anything before seen in MoD, but was soon to be surpassed...

AMSO had previously introduced a policy of 'Just in Time', whereby stocks were reduced to levels that assumed a spare would arrive on the shelf just as a demand came in. Predictably, this didn't work out (as they controlled little of the process), wasting even more money; again because the policy required more frequent buys, in smaller quantities, increasing the unit price. They again faced having to find a way of concealing the waste.

In September 1990, and without notifying anyone, a 'Not in Time' policy was introduced. Instead of spares arriving just in time, requisitions to procure or repair would only be raised when there was an outstanding demand. That is, after Depot Stock, Contingency and War Reserves ran out (whether through being used, or scrapped). The policy was revealed when faulty test equipment halted surveillance radar repair work. High priority demands from front line couldn't be met; exposed immediately during Transition to War. AMSO found themselves unable to supply kit that should have been sat in store at immediate readiness. Front line and the media criticised politicians for unpreparedness and lack of funding. Those responsible stayed silent.

In February 1991 an Equipment Accounting Centre (EAC) audit report criticised AMSO's position on DM87 as *'untenable'*.[14] Copied to Contracts

---

14 Acs EAC 1E AIRTC, 19 February 1991. Audit report 'Embodiment Loan holdings at Air Transport Charter (Ltd)'.

Policy, it emphasised the need for a policy-level resolution. No reply was received or action taken, the first indication of a major change that was being quietly planned - the project managers who had challenged DM87 were to be transferred to AMSO on 1 April 1992. They would then be complaining about their own superiors, and subject to disciplinary action and detriment for refusing to commit fraud. And so it proved.

But, inevitably, the pressure told. AMSO had increasingly awkward questions to answer. Initially, at Air Commodore level it was asked how and by whom the waste had been identified. Answer - civilian engineers had conducted Requirement Scrutiny. Ask any reasonable person what should happen now, and they'll reply: *Direct AMSO to conduct Requirement Scrutiny in accordance with mandated policy.*

AMSO had a choice to make. Help or hinder. On 5 February 1992 their staff were told they were to <u>no longer conduct Requirement Scrutiny</u>. Issuing a directive to conduct scrutiny correctly would be to concede it hadn't been; admitting serious offences. This illegal order was two big fingers to the Permanent Under-Secretary of State and, more importantly, front line.

Wrapped in a tight cocoon of inertia and apathy, and confusing their rank with the Permanent Under-Secretary's authority, these senior officers sought to prevent future challenges. On the same day, RAF and civilian supply staff were instructed that they should only communicate with project offices at their own level. Every phone call began with: *'What grade are you?'*. The replies came as a shock to their Wing Commanders and Squadron Leaders, who found themselves inundated with questions *they* now had to ask of the engineers, who had hitherto been happy to accept them from whoever had the query.

But there was obviously internal disagreement. On 21 February 1992 SS51(RAF) sought the removal of electronic spares from the excluded range list.

'Not surprisingly, repair costs have risen steeply in proportion to the cost of the item, due to contractors being forced into buying small batch quantities of repair spares. Repair turn-round-times have increased considerably and managers' time expended on small value problems have reached unacceptable levels'.[15]

This was interesting, because SS51 managed consumables, not

---

15 D/ADSS 51(RAF/421/3/38, 21 February 1992.

repairables. Within AMSO they had borne the brunt of industry complaints, and were now making it known who was really responsible. But the replacements for what had been scrapped would still have to be bought; which would still take at least three years. It had taken over four years to accept what had been notified on 13 January 1988.

The RAF officer who wrote this admission, a Wing Commander, deserves huge praise. He had inherited the situation and made an immediate decision that his superiors, and other supply branches, were wrong. And he had the courtesy to copy his letter (to SMS81, a policy branch) to the project managers who, for these four years, had been subject to detriment by his superiors for saying precisely the same thing. But he was 'only' a Wing Commander; there were still four higher levels of rank to persuade, and multiple advocates of the waste at each. And none of his colleagues at his rank agreed with him - at least not publicly.

Perhaps reflecting the internal reaction to a supply officer supporting the project managers, a few weeks later, on 24 March 1992, the *speak at your own level* directive was rescinded, replaced with *All queries are to be sent direct to the project managers' boss*, a Group Captain equivalent; immediately inundating *him*.

Infinitely worse, upon the MoD(PE) project managers transferring to AMSO on 1 April 1992 the first edict issued was that, henceforth, any administrator would have superiority over any civilian engineer, irrespective of grade. The project managers now had line managers who were up to three grades below them. This is called bullying and harassment.

Following a summer of discontent, on 4 September 1992 a directive was issued that forthwith supply officers must deal with companies at two levels above that of 'their' project managers. Industry's reaction was universal - if AMSO wanted to change the terms of the contracts, send in a proposal and they would provide an (increased) quote.

This was getting farcical, not to mention puerile, especially the RAF's preoccupation with rank; and most civilian suppliers agreed. But in a Service organisation, where one cannot be wrong by virtue of one's rank, *they* could be ignored. The conscious fraud and waste continued unabated. MoD's name was dragged through the gutter, all for want of a bit of common sense.

Failure to conduct knowledgeable Requirement Scrutiny, and its intersection with the policy of *savings at the expense of safety*, was the critical juncture, the nexus point. Nor were they true *savings*, which do not impact operational effectiveness. Despite Mr Haddon-Cave's claim of 1998, the policy had already gained momentum by 1988.

Once these failings had been notified and ignored, they became violations. They persisted, and by 2001 personnel seeking transfer or advancement were being asked questions at interview to ensure they understood that safety concerns, waste and fraud should be overlooked in order to avoid upsetting the perpetrators. At this point the engineers were advised to retain copies of all correspondence for legal reasons - which most, and certainly those with airworthiness delegation, had been doing for a decade anyway.

And hence, the detailed evidence to the Nimrod and Mull of Kintyre Reviews. Which, I'm pretty sure, Secretary of State Des Browne didn't expect when waiving the Official Secrets Act for those wishing to speak to the former, putting it in the public domain for the latter. The delicious irony was not lost on some. The former RAF Chief Engineer from 1991-96, who was double-hatted as Air Member Logistics from 1994-96, had been in post more or less throughout this period of prodigious waste, and had ignored the Director of Flight Safety, was and remains one of the most vocal opponents of the Mull of Kintyre Review findings. He was hoisted by his failure to carry out his sworn duty; although he was by no means the worst.

Childish things

On avionics, matters came to a head when RAF suppliers refused to attend RN Production and Repair progress meetings if the RN were present. Instead, they would wait for the meeting to be held, and the following day a posse would turn up at the company and demand they ignore all actions placed the previous day.

(Around the same time a Wing Commander from SM47(RAF) was invited to leave Ferranti Radar Systems in Edinburgh when he turned up unannounced and started haranguing the company, and threatening and verbally abusing his project manager 'colleague').

The matter was raised formally on 10 September 1992. A project manager, while conducting scrutiny, had noted the equipment was not needed. It was a minor error. The wrong box had been ticked by the RN's Ranging and Scaling Group. Test equipment was being bought for every ship in the Navy, but it was only used at the 3rd Line workshop at the Royal Naval Aircraft Yard, Fleetlands, who already had theirs. Such errors are relatively common, and easily spotted and fixed. If MoD doesn't, companies probably will. They know that if MoD spends its money on the wrong thing, there's nothing left for the right thing, and everyone's reputation will suffer. (A concept often ignored by their critics). The RAF demanded that the company, Thorn-EMI in Crawley, accept the contract and build the equipment. They refused.

The RAF's own contracts branch then wrote to the company on 14 September 1992:

'(Supply Management Branches) have no authority to call any meeting on your contracts. You are not obliged to receive their attendance on your premises. Should you agree to, you should advise them beforehand that they shall be presented with an invoice for the cost of the meeting and that payment shall be made in full on the day'.[16]

And simultaneously, to the suppliers:

'(You) have no authority to call any meeting for which SM(AV/PDS)4(RAF) (the project management branch) *or CB/SM21B3(RAF) are the Technical and Contractual Authority. If you insist, you shall be presented with a bill for the cost, and the contractor will insist on immediate payment'.*

Ignoring this, the suppliers turned up on 7 October, demanding to hold a progress meeting on a non-existent contract. A formal complaint was lodged that day by the company's Managing Director.

In this particular case the suppliers had committed fraud, twice. First, they had raised a number of Local Purchase Orders (LPO), sending them to Thorn-EMI, who notified the project manager. These are for low value items or tasks which would otherwise clog up the contracts loop. The total 'requirement' was far in excess of the LPO limit. It had been broken down into smaller chunks: strictly forbidden and each, rather obviously, a Requirement Scrutiny failure. Second, they had sent a duplicate requirement to a project office in MoD(PE) (SLR22A), asking them to buy the equipment; revealing intent to deceive. This had slipped through the Thorn-EMI system and was being delivered, and would promptly be scrapped under DM87. The clear aim was to bypass their own contracts branch, and the project managers who were identifying this fraud. The RAF's Director Contracts sought a briefing.

---

16 Fax from CB/SM21B3(RAF) to Thorn-EMI Electronics Ltd, 14 September 1992.

It was submitted on 9 October 1992, and finished:

'How much equipment is being bought this way without knowledgeable scrutiny? To stand back and do nothing is not on'.

He concurred, and on 14 October 1992 the responsible Assistant Director Contracts formally endorsed the actions of his own staff and the project management branches.[17] The suppliers' reaction was to escalate. A decision had been made at the most senior level in AMSO. These civilian engineers and contracts officers had to be stopped once and for all. Their behaviour was not to be tolerated.

On 8 December 1992 Director General Support Management (RAF), Air Vice Marshal Christopher Baker, visited London with two Air Commodores in tow, and threatened <u>his own</u> civilian project managers - primarily MoD's airworthiness and simulator specialists - with dismissal should they persist in their refusal to waste money. The policy directive of 5 February 1992 was reiterated - they would <u>not</u> conduct Requirement Scrutiny. Baker's concern? His supply staff had been caught committing fraud, and he had <u>personally</u> approved their actions - which he reiterated at the hearing. Being the 2-Star in charge of <u>all</u> aviation support, he had made AMSO's formal position clear to all.

But his mistake was to assume these civilian staff would just roll over and take his bullying. Instead, they asked Director Internal Audit (DIA) in Bath to conduct an audit into Requirement Scrutiny practices; and more to the point, maladministration and fraud. DIA reported to the Permanent Under-Secretary of State in June 1996, concluding:

'We are unable to provide an assurance to PUS that Requirement Scrutiny is operating effectively in all areas'.

The main recommendation repeated a mandate:

'That system provisioning parameters are reviewed periodically and evidence retained of the review'. [18]

Whose job had this been? The now defunct Provisioning Authorities.

When the report was issued (and those threatened by Baker were sent personal copies) my 2-Star in MoD(PE) was Director General Air Systems 2 (DGAS2). I soon had an opportunity to speak to him about it,

---

17 Loose Minute D/ADC SM2(RAF)/3/1, 14 October 1992.
18 Report D/DIA/5/295/10, 27 June 1996. 'Requirement Scrutiny'.

asking why we had heard nothing from senior management about the 19 recommendations. He replied: *'The report is of no concern to MoD(PE)'*. To say this he would have to enjoy support from the Chief of Defence Procurement, responsible for the Defence equipment budget which DIA had just reported was being flushed down the toilet. The report was destroyed after seven years, because it was not implemented; confirmed by DIA on 15 October 2007.[19]

In case you think this subject (avionic production and support) small beer, the <u>recurring</u> annual waste on avionics alone ran to well over £100M (~£250M in 2023) - and Director Internal Audit confirmed the failings were pan-MoD. By contrast, maintaining the build standard for <u>all</u> avionics cost around £13M per year (mostly man-hours). In an effort to offset the cost of DM87, this pot was robbed of ~28% each year between 1991 and 1994; making little inroads but decimating safety. Compounding this, the 1991 inflation rate was 5.9%, and the Department of Trade and Industry index for aviation (the actual funding increase required to maintain the status quo) was almost double that; meaning the real cuts were nearer 40%.

DM87 and Not in Time were pebbles thrown in a pond long ago, and the ripples are still extending. What these procurers did was meet a legal obligation to refuse to obey illegal orders, and report fraud and incitement to commit fraud. Others in MoD jumped on the bandwagon. In 2001 DGAS2 (by now renamed Executive Director 1) confirmed it remained an offence to refuse to obey an order to make a false declaration that Requirement Scrutiny had been carried out.[20] This was upheld, twice, by the Chief of Defence Procurement.[21] Prospect, the Trades Union representing most project managers, issued a notification of the ruling.[22]

On numerous occasions between 2000 and 2012 the policy was queried by MPs; particularly Steve Webb, in whose constituency many MoD employees at MoD AbbeyWood lived. MoD's replies were consistent, including a briefing to the Under Secretary of State on 23 April 2003, later released under Freedom of Information. The policy stood.

---

19 Letter D/DIA(Bath)/6/5/2, 15 October 2007.
20 Letter XD1(304), 10 January 2001.
21 Letters CDP 117/6/7, 19 November 2001 and 13 December 2001.
22 Letter DPA/C175/JF/62/02, 18 September 2002.

On 16 February 2012 Margaret Hodge MP, chair of the Public Accounts Committee, was notified of the rulings and ongoing waste. The Clerk of the committee replied, saying Mrs Hodge had asked for the notification to be circulated to all members. Progress was sought in August and September 2012, but the committee did not reply. It remains silent, and no report it has issued mentions the subject. Yet its website proclaims:

'The Public Accounts Committee examines the value for money of Government projects, programmes and service delivery. Drawing on the work of the National Audit Office the Committee holds government officials to account for the economy, efficiency and effectiveness of public spending'.

But not, it seems, MoD officials or Ministers.

Finally, Sir Jeremy Heywood, Cabinet Secretary and Head of the Civil Service, ruled on 28 October 2014 it would be *'inappropriate'* to rescind disciplinary action taken against staff for refusing to obey these illegal orders. No action was taken against those who issued the orders, threatened staff, and handed down punishments. Financial probity was one genie that had made quite enough trouble, and was now pushed firmly back into its box.

All this may sound utterly bizarre to you; but I have cited the letter references. In fact, the two Chief of Defence Procurement references were taken from the aforementioned Ministerial Briefing prepared for him by the Director of Personnel, Resources and Development. At no time has MoD sought to deny these events occurred. It simply states that the only *'wrongdoing'* was the refusal to obey the order to commit fraud.

Essentially, this is the background to the Nimrod Review. It was MoD's refusal to budge from its position that provoked my notifications to Ministers, Oxford Coroner Andrew Walker, and the Review; in that order. (The Review commenced before the Inquest, but the Coroner and his Clerk of the Court, Geoff Webb, took submissions before the Review was announced). Only Messrs Walker and Webb acted correctly and with due diligence.

Mr Haddon-Cave did say, correctly, that if money had not been wasted the post-Strategic Defence Review 1998 *'financial targets'* (20% over five years) would have been more easily achieved without compromising airworthiness. He omitted that this 4% per year was swamped by the ~28% per year from 1991-94, directly targeting airworthiness; and that the waste far exceeded the cost of doing the job properly. *Who benefitted?*

II

THE WASTE

My approach is to set out the *39 Steps* within their seven groupings, discuss who is required to be able to answer them, and why, and offer case studies and the occasional anecdote.

Please don't get hung up on *where* I place these, as a requirement can fail scrutiny for more than one reason. Where I've put them is merely a reflection of the way I look at that particular event, what the first warning sign was, or (primarily) for continuity purposes. All are fully documented, and some were used in the main submissions to the Nimrod and Mull of Kintyre Reviews (2007-2011).

Group 1 - Types, Numbers and Duplication

1. *Why is it needed?*

2. *What will it do?*

3. *What is the threat, is it new, different or the same?*

4. *Do we need it at all? If so, how soon?*

5. *Is it a new equipment or a replacement? If the latter, how many do we have of the current equipment, when does it become obsolete, and what are the running costs?*

6. *How many do we need, what reliability is being aimed for, what is the spares requirement? Are these affordable?*

7. *Is there any relationship with other equipments and if so, are the timescales consistent?*

8. *Are there any alternatives and, if so, would they be any cheaper?*

9. *Has the requirement been overstated (possibly so as to fix on a particular solution)? If so, is there any acceptable change which would allow competition?*

The answers to #1-4 form the basis of the requirement, circulated by the Directorate of Equipment Capability for comment and initial internal Service approval. The Provisioning Authority will at this stage have answered #5-9; and must thereafter be able to answer all.

Warning signs

An Urgent Operational Requirement was approved for a top-up buy of Radar Warning Receivers (RWR) for RN Commando helicopters being deployed to a conflict zone. But with independent scrutiny now forbidden, and the RN having got rid of its corporate knowledge, a simplistic statement had been made - *There's not enough, we need more.*

Under normal circumstances the specialist RWR office would be given the job. But in the first indication something was amiss, the requirement was sent instead to the aircraft project office. Plainly, someone wanted to avoid closer scrutiny.

Commander (Air) at the Royal Naval Air Station Yeovilton confirmed to the project manager that less than one third of his aircraft were now fitted, and he desperately needed the kit. Both knew sufficient had been procured to meet the Fit Policy, so where was it? Working through the approvals chain, someone soon got antsy. *Butt out, just spend the money.* You know you're on target when the flak hits.

To save money, the repair contract had not been renewed. Unserviceable kit was languishing at the company, and MoD was paying for its storage. To conceal this, the 'solution' was to buy new; but there were still no repairs planned. Expensive and fully repairable kit was now deemed consumable. The project manager refused to let a new contract.

Space in the aircraft was at a premium, and the Processor/Power Supply Unit had been positioned under a seat, the cooling intake facing inboard. Now, troops get bored, and probably quite nervous, in the back of helicopters. They have a predisposition to poking their bayonets into any nearby orifice. The main 'fault' was bayonet insertion into the cooling intake, breaking the fan. In reliability and liability terms that doesn't count as a failure; but the removal and replacement of the damaged equipment still places a demand on logistic support.

Solution - stop playing with your bayonet. Poke it somewhere else, or in someone else, not in something costing north of £100k. A routine repair contract was needed, and a quiet word.

The project manager went to the company, Racal Radar in Leicester, and looked at their survey sheets; which revealed (unsurprisingly) that the same spares were required to effect each repair; but there were none in stock and they had no contractual cover to buy any. Solution? Provide cover and buy them. Ignoring the endorsed requirement, he did just that and quickly the aircraft were fitted again, at a cost of around £100k. The approved requirement would have taken two years and £xxM.

Front line were of course delighted, but the others furious at their maladministration being revealed. They needn't have worried. Onward and upward, when what was needed was their delegations withdrawn and never returned. Harsh? I don't think so. Often, similar events are simple errors or oversights. But a quite deliberate decision was made to send the requirement to a different project office, hoping they didn't know the background and would just let a contract. That revealed intent.

How did the project manager know what to do? First, and obviously, he knew to conduct Requirement Scrutiny. Second, he knew Commander

(Air). Third, his previous job had been in the Directorate that *should* have been given the job, and knew who to ask about current status. The first should be a given, but is not. But the others were pure luck. It needed all three to align to get the right result.

Goodbye sweet dreams

Aircrew suffer from noise-induced hearing loss. The obvious waste occurs if they have to be medically downgraded or even discharged. Less obviously, they can be compensated financially. Is this avoidable?

There are two types of noise to consider - damaging and annoying. Both are equally important, the latter crucial in aircraft where total concentration is required for the entire mission. In 1997 the world's first fully integrated Active Noise Reduction (ANR) system was fitted to one such aircraft, Sea King AEW Mk2; described by the RN's test and evaluation experts at Boscombe Down as the *'greatest advance in aircrew safety since the ejection seat'*. (Admittedly they were helicopter crews, who tend not to use ejection seats). Research and development cost £1M, each helmet modification set under £800. Compare that to the cost of training replacement aircrew, and (typically) ~£250k compensation.[23]

Also, ANR provided a 78% increase in sonar audio detection range, when MoD historically spent ~£3M every 18 months squeezing low single figure gains via software. This can be read across to other uses where hearing is important or at risk, such as submarines and groundcrew. On a lighter note, this was the first time these RN sonics experts would admit the Sea King system was better than the old Wessex.

Against this background, on 1 October 2007 the Nimrod Integrated Project Team (IPT) issued Invitation to Tender (ITT) NIMES/5362. The tender document was 43 pages, with the actual requirement articulated in less than half a page.

Nimrod had procured Racal/Thales Atlantic RA155/2004 headsets with ANR modules, but now realised they could not be used because there was no Headset Interface Box or cables of any kind, and the headsets had the wrong plug. A complete failure of scrutiny and absence of fact checking. The ITT now sought to correct this, seeking bids to:

---

23 https://industrialclaims.co.uk/

- Design, Manufacture and Supply a replacement Headset Interface Box (LRU 8022). *(No quantity stated).*
- Production of a new rack of mounting brackets for LRU 8022. *(No quantity stated).*
- Re-termination of Headsets *(i.e. procure and fit the proper plug).*
- Production of 100 *black* ANR headset extension cables (curly lead).
- Production of 25 *red* ANR Flight Deck crew Headset Interface Cables (curly lead).
- Production of 25 *yellow* Flight Deck crew Headset Interface Cables (curly lead). *(No specification was provided for any lead).*

But the Invitation to Tender omitted:

- How was the system to be powered, battery or from the aircraft? If the latter (in practice the intercom), who was being contracted to modify that, and would there be a directed sub-contract? This was particularly important because the existing *'curly leads'* were 4-core (mic/tels), but may now have to be 6-core to include power. That would increase weight, in turn requiring a check that the headsets stayed on one's head.
- How long were the *'curly leads'* to be, when extended?
- How *'curly'* were they to be? (6-core roughly doubles the curled diameter, in turn affecting stowage of what is a tripping hazard).
- The requirement was for Flight Deck crew only. Was this deliberate? It is a common mistake; Merlin having made it in reverse some years earlier, concentrating on passengers (troops) in the rear when aircrew were subjected to the higher dose.
- Would MoD be supplying drawings?
- Was the simulator to be modified? Crew must be trained to deal with an ANR failure, trials having shown this makes the pilot duck as the sudden noise is startling.
- What was the intercom, and would MoD supply the Interface Definition and Interface Control Documents? And was it clear or secure? That is, was the ANR system to be TEMPEST cleared? (Communications Security, to prevent unwanted electronic emissions. A code name, not an acronym). This was especially important as Nimrod had procured a secure intercom costing over

£50M, *but had decided not to fit it.* (How did that pass scrutiny?) Allied to this, if TEMPEST clearance was required then the Headset/ANR module became a Line Replaceable Unit of the intercom, as well as an Aircrew Equipment Assembly.

- As Nimrod didn't have a valid Safety Case, how could bidders satisfy the requirement to update it?

These issues (and you'll be pleased to hear I won't spell them out like this in every case study), which should have been addressed during initial scrutiny and tender preparation, were the primary cost drivers. Any bid omitting them would, by definition, be a fraction of the true cost. Any bidder who did not ask these questions would be unsuitable.

The only question the IPT was able to answer was to provide an outline drawing for the existing bracket. It denied knowing what a clear intercom was, saying it didn't recognise the term. It did eventually agree TEMPEST clearance was required, giving lie to the clear intercom claim. But would not say who would be embodying the prerequisite secure intercom, when, or even what it was. Was it the one already bought for £50M? Did it even know of its existence, languishing in stores?

TEMPEST would be the most expensive activity, with the IPT required to arrange that Government Communications Headquarters (GCHQ) carry out assessments and testing at every stage. (TEMPEST is a Home Office policy imposed on MoD, the highly classified specification prone to change). The ITT did not mention security classification.

One company who responded were vetronics specialists. It happened they employed a retired Squadron Leader as a consultant, who had worked on Nimrod MR1 as an Engineering Officer, in MoD(PE) on Nimrod R1, and at Boscombe Down managing Tornado trials. He was appointed bid manager and submitted the above questions. MoD's responses were piecemeal, and increasingly prickly. The Nimrod contracts officer, NIM(ES) Comm MS1, finally snapped, submitting a complaint to the company directors about the bid manager's *'attitude'*, ignoring that his questions were both perfectly reasonable and helpful. The company were excluded, effectively blacklisted.

I've listed eight valid questions from just one company. The IPT claimed that, between them, the other bidders had only asked <u>one</u> question, relating to one of them not having the latest version of Defence Standard 00-970, the Design and Airworthiness Requirements for

Service Aircraft. (Download it from MoD's website!)

If MoD let the contract based on its ITT, the 'winning' bidder would inevitably call a halt at some point, and submit a quote for the additional work. Plainly, no scrutiny had taken place. Moreover, Nimrod had procured a proprietary ANR system, not realising, or ignoring, that MoD owned the Intellectual Property Rights to a system that not only met the legal noise dose limit of 85dB(A), but had achieved 73dB(A).

If this was the standard of work tolerated by the RAF support organisation, then little wonder Nimrod was in trouble.

An ANR system must be tailored for the noise in each application. It is essential that aircrew must still be able to hear audio cues such as warning tones and mechanical clunks and grinding; whereas it is acceptable to give 'passive' users in other applications a simple broadband system that reduces noise across the entire spectrum. For this reason the MoD-owned system was reconfigurable (via software) for target frequencies; even for different seats in the aircraft.

In addition to audio cues, the effect of the ANR on the Existing Aircraft System must be assessed. Does it change its performance in any way? The answer is normally yes, typically manifesting as a dulling of the tels (telephone, or what you hear) if there is a failure, or if someone is not wearing an ANR headset or helmet. *That's* where ANR money goes. Assessment, Demonstration and Safety.

So, how was the Atlantic's ANR module selected? Had the Integrated Project Team tested and verified it in a representative environment? Was there a Certificate of Design and Performance relating to its use in Nimrod? Asked and answered, because MoD couldn't provide one.

Has this ever proven to be a problem? I mentioned the loss of seven aircrew in the 2003 Sea King mid-air. It emerged in 2010, after MoD was questioned by one family, that four had the wrong helmet. Communications quality in each aircraft would have been severely degraded. The main procedural issue raised by the Board of Inquiry had been: *Why were they not communicating with each other?* But it did not attempt to answer its own question, its report presenting absence of evidence as evidence of absence, implying the crews had not tried. It omitted that a critical risk had been properly mitigated by the *programme* manager; and then de-mitigated by a non-technical superior. Knowing this, the RN and Integrated Project Team contributed by allowing aircrew to use whatever helmet they liked, when a specific build standard was mandated on safety and performance grounds. As these actions were taken knowing of the immediate risk to life they caused, I regard the deaths as corporate manslaughter.

Pull through

MoD used to commit a tidy sum to Research and Development. It had superb scientists, who would work alongside industry on ground-breaking advances. The primary vehicle was Applied Research Packages (ARP), run from Main Building. The problem was 'pull through'. How did procurers know what science there was to apply?

While I said ANR was delivered in 1997, the basic design was ready in the mid-80s, delivered under an ARP for RAF Harriers. Main Building finished the ARP, filed it away, and began another one. The system had worked, up to a point, but nobody had taken advantage because there was no mechanism to tell Operational Requirements and project managers there was now a solution to a long-standing risk. Of course, this was pre-internet and e-mail, which arrived in MoD in July 1996. You needed to know someone who knew a man. Or make a phone call.

As part of the preliminary work in 1996, senior staff were advised again of the benefits of a database of ARP outputs, and making it accessible on the new MoD(PE) intranet. One would simply type 'noise reduction', and be able to download all relevant data. The suggestion was taken up, making subsequent failures all the more puzzling.

Obsolescent or obsolete?

1996. The Apache Attack Helicopter project office was contracting fully fitted aircraft, the Army waiving through the avionic fit proposed by the US. A project manager in the same Directorate asked the Project Director if it was to be marinised for operating off carriers, pointing out the *onboard commonality* requirement. The answer was yes, and he asked to see the aircraft specification. It revealed the US were off-loading kit removed from older Apaches during an upgrade. Some of it had been considered obsolescent for over 15 years. For example, Bendix RT221 VHF radios, whose repair policy had been 'repair by cannibalisation' since 1980. And Apache was expecting a further 30+ years support...

The Project Director declared planning blight. He had to. The avionics fit in a modern aircraft is hugely expensive. At the time, a Sea Harrier radar cost about 40% that of the airframe. The V/UHF radio used in Sea King, Lynx and Merlin around £130k. This sounds extortionate, but try asking Sony how much they'd charge to design and build 100 bespoke TVs, to a military specification, incorporating features that are UK EYES ONLY, with no potential for further sales. Ever. They'd laugh, but their best guess would be a couple of million each.

'Commercial Off-The-Shelf' the committees cry. That V/UHF multimode radio? There's part of the design our closest allies aren't allowed to know about, although they know we have the capability it provides. As do they in *their* equivalent. Newsflash. Amazon doesn't sell them. The upshot was the Apache contract was changed from 'aircraft' to 'air vehicles', leaving the project office to resolve the avionics issue.

Why did scrutiny, *from the customer's point of view*, for a £4.1Bn buy of 67 aircraft, miss this entirely, when it was spotted immediately by someone unconnected with the programme, saving years of delay and untold millions? One obstacle the Project Director faced was that Apache had an extraordinary 73 Army personnel working on Logistics Support, but he didn't manage them. They came under Master-General of the Ordnance. As *they* had the avionic specialists, the Project Director had none of his own.

This prompted his Director, responsible for all helicopters except Merlin, to label the errant project manager *'an embarrassment to the department'*, telling him to move out of Air Systems. It wasn't clear why he was subjected to this detriment, but it is likely the Executive Board were unhappy at him exposing scrutiny failure. But quietly, and without advertising the posts, two Army officers and two civilians were appointed to a newly created Apache avionics section. They never knew why their posts had been created.

However, Apache was still years late...

Private stash

The Conservative government of John Major introduced the Private Finance Initiative (PFI) in 1992. This uses the private sector to deliver public sector infrastructure and/or services to a public sector specification; the defining characteristic being the use of private sector debt and equity, underwritten by the public. It was intended for hospitals, roads and the like. The cost is repaid over an agreed period, say 25 years. If MoD decides to remove the equipment/facility from service before then, it still has to pay up. (To limit the damage it is sensible to negotiate contract 'exit points'). Put another way, the government may boast a Defence equipment budget of £xxBn per year, but one must subtract fixed PFI payments before committing anything else. Value for money? The National Audit Office thought so. Detractors saw it as expensive hand-out to the private sector, creative accounting at the expense of front line capability. In 2009 it was revealed by the trade association for PFI firms that 630 schemes had been put in place since 1992, covering investment of £63Bn. The remaining repayments, between 2009 and 2033, would cost the country £217Bn, variable with the inflation rate.

A prime PFI target was aircraft simulators, and training in general. At precisely the same time Apache was 'encouraged' to PFI its simulator, Sea King ASaC Mk7 was *instructed* to PFI its Full Mission Trainer. Asked for advice, the Directorate's contracts staff were stumped. And to add context, this was but one of many 'initiatives' being thrown at them; including MoD(PE)'s new project management and personnel spying software system, ASPECT; deemed the highest priority task, with at any time half the staff away on training courses. (Later quietly scrapped, incurring huge waste). However, upon obtaining and studying the PFI 'rules' the contracts manager circulated a 'tick sheet', revealing under what circumstances PFI could be *avoided*. One box said 'Overseas Sales'. If none were envisaged, then one could opt out.

The Sea King manager based his decision on the fact only one other country, Spain, flew the AEW, and they used the RN's existing Trainer at the Royal Naval Air Station Culdrose, in Cornwall. He procured his Trainer outright. (That the RN hadn't asked for it is a different issue, and I've dealt with the reason). The cost was offset by a little known tax device whereby aircraft under a certain tonnage are exempt from VAT. Even Westland were unaware of this, so think how much of the Defence budget has been handed to the Inland Revenue over the decades... Tongue in cheek, Westland suggested rebates going back to 1947.

But, despite dire warnings that the In Service Date would be delayed by years (because one cannot declare it until a given number of aircraft are operational, which tends to require trained pilots), Apache PFI'd their simulator. There would now be a 3-year delay. Initial Operating Capability for what was supposed to be a simple build-to-print job was declared in October 2004, and aircrew training took place over the next three years. It is unclear how many UK build standard simulators were sold overseas, but the figure is generally thought to be less than one.

Bad enough. But when Westland started to deliver the aircraft they had to be placed in storage, and a system of aircraft husbandry established to keep them in reasonable shape. This was compounded by needing the hangar space for Lynx and Merlin programmes. (Eventually, they were stored at an MoD site). MoD had a solution. Another cunning plan. It demanded of Westland they cut the production rate in half, but at nil-cost to MoD; meaning it could transfer blame to the company. Whoever thought that one up was unhinged, and of course Westland said no. (I'm being polite).

In 2018 Chancellor of the Exchequer Philip Hammond (and Defence Secretary between 2011-14) announced that the UK government would no longer use PFI. The predictions of the 1990s were proving true, departments such as the NHS sleep-walking into costly disputes as their PFI contracts started expiring - many of them including final exit payments of many millions. What was off-book, was now very much on-book, and eating up budgets before a penny could be spent.

The real Sir Humphrey

While on Apache, a few comments on a Public Accounts Committee hearing of 24 October 2004, the subject being 'Battlefield Helicopters'. MoD lead was Permanent Under-Secretary of State Sir Kevin Tebbit. When asked about aircrew training he replied:

'I have not come prepared to discuss Apache, as this is not a hearing on Apache'.

If Apache is not a Battlefield Helicopter, what is it?

He was then asked about the Army Air Corps' recent contribution to the Allied Rapid Reaction Force, whereby their deployment to Iraq had to be by ship, not air, losing 21 days training time. Also, their general lack of resources. Sir Kevin replied:

'I think they were hampered by the short notice...'.

Can it truly be a *Rapid* Reaction Force if it is not sufficiently resourced to be *rapid*?

There are 30 pages of the same, but the issues were best summed up by Angela Browning MP (now Baroness Browning):

'It is alright to procure the machines, but obviously that is not the only part of the picture; it is whether there are sufficient properly trained people able to

carry out sufficient flying hours to be adequately trained.

In other words: why did the Defence Lines of Development break down, and why did Apache pass Requirement Scrutiny with such obvious shortfalls in resourcing?

Fools rush in

I've just mentioned a V/UHF multimode radio, the AD3400. MoD bought around 700, costing over £90M. In time, another application was identified, and the aircraft project manager delivered the comms system and aircraft installation designs. The aircraft were to have two each, at nil-cost because a surplus of around 160 existed due to fleet reductions. Put another way, any attempt to buy more radios, or a different type of radio, would fail *Step #4*, as the approval was predicated on use of this surplus. The system had worked correctly, so far.

On the verge of fitting the new systems, the project manager was told to buy a different radio, from Elmer in Italy. His line manager, an administrator, instructed him to make a false declaration that there was no surplus, and sign Technical and Financial Approval. He refused point blank to commit this fraud, and his outrageous insubordination was reported to a senior RN officer. At the disciplinary hearing he explained that if the RN now wanted Elmer (they'd firmly said they <u>didn't</u>), the 'requirement' would have to be resubmitted for approval, and the project start over. That, the scrutineer would ask why the senior officer's staff (not the RN) now proposed buying a lesser radio, when the formal endorsement was to use a surplus of a higher specification radio.

The senior officer knew all this to be true - 12 years earlier he'd been the RN HQ desk officer on Lynx. Instead, he claimed he had authorised the entire surplus to be scrapped. Quite apart from not having that authority (far too senior!), this was an outright lie as the project manager had already arranged for the radios to be quarantined at the Design Authority, ready to be inspected, tested, and form part of the installation kits. The following day he uncovered another 13, languishing at a workshop under a temporary NATO Stock Number. £1.7M worth of assets, just like that. But even if the claim had been true, the project manager was still correct in his actions because the new unendorsed requirement failed scrutiny, and significant extra funding was required.

Ignoring all this, a formal warning was issued as to his future conduct; and outside the hearing was 'advised' to find another job. With a serious charge now sitting on his record, and constructively dismissed from post, either of which would at a stroke prevent advancement (and so it proved), he sought redress for this detriment. Long story short, his appeal was rejected at 2 and 4-Star level within MoD, by three Defence Ministers, and two Cabinet Secretaries.

Hang on to your mobiles

To a foot or vehicle patrol, especially in mountainous terrain, long range comms is achieved by High Frequency (HF) radio, which 'bounces' the signal off the ionosphere. (Satellite communication is a possibility, but access is limited and assets scarce). Good HF frequencies tend to last 10-15 minutes due to changing atmospheric conditions. Hence, the military employs a frequency prediction methodology, and signallers are given around 20-30 predicted frequencies, often a month in advance. These are pre-programmed into the radio, which 'polls' and ranks them. By definition this requires the radio to transmit, eating up battery power and letting the enemy know where you are. The difficulty faced by users is obvious, especially if none of the predicted frequencies work.

This dilemma was one of the Operational Constraints that BOWMAN was required to resolve; a £2.5Bn programme begun in the 1980s, which came to fruition in the late-00s. But in anticipation of it being unfit for purpose (!), a project had been approved in 1999 to replace or enhance its HF component with a Low Probability of Intercept/Low Probability of Detection system. That is: reduce or eliminate the need to poll, and 99.5% of messages must get through first time (against the current achievement of around 3%). It cannot be overemphasised how extraordinary this was - a formal requirement based on the premise that a £2.5Bn programme wouldn't be good enough was political dynamite. And as soon as this requirement (Project VISIGOTH) was endorsed, BOWMAN HF failed Requirement Scrutiny and should have been returned for reappraisal. It wasn't, much to the relief of the Army office who had signed both requirements.

VISIGOTH was embarrassment. Even when due to arrive *after* BOWMAN, it was such a hot potato the BOWMAN team refused to even acknowledge it. At first intended for 'specialist' units, it was given to a 'specialist' team. However, again, everyone gave it a body swerve, because it would bring one into immediate conflict with superiors, who would be furious if delivered *before* BOWMAN. Then 9/11 happened, war broke out in Afghanistan, and the casualty rate increased for want of the capability.

In 2003 the new Communications, Intelligence, Surveillance and Reconnaissance Integrated Project Team Leader decided he needed someone with nothing to lose, and approached an experienced engineer who was working part-time due to serious health issues. Asked if he knew how to proceed, he replied the basic solution was already in service with the RN and RAF, and would speak to Marlborough Communications Ltd about tailoring it for this Army requirement. The immediate lesson being the existing capability was not identified during scrutiny, indicating the wrong people conducted it. Point proven when a random project manager can take one look and say what the solution is. Four years had been wasted.

Shortly after taking up post, the project manager was instructed to cancel the project as *'it involves integration and that is too risky'*. (The team leader was unaware of this directive). This revealed much about the speaker's background, complete lack of experience and suitability, and the system that permitted him to be in such a position. Luckily, he was ignored. Time on the ANN system had already been booked. (Anglo-Norwegian-Netherlands comms relay, used to test such systems). That week, a Warrant Officer was extracted from theatre and flown back to the UK for trials, which were successful beyond expectations. Fifteen sets (ample for the unit involved) were loaned free of charge and deployed to Afghanistan in September 2003, three weeks before the main BOWMAN contract was let.

Having delivered, the project manager now had to seek approval to *initiate* the project. (The second example of this I've mentioned). And, of course, deal with those seething at life-saving capability being delivered ahead of time, under cost, and to a better specification. At the time, MoD had abandoned its relatively efficient delegation and approvals system, and 15 people in the Integrated Project Team now had to read and approve his plans. Fourteen were reasonably quick, most admitting they didn't understand the issues so simply rubber-stamped. (You might well ask why they had this role). However, the last was on extended leave and due back in five weeks. When he returned, his only comment was the project manager had typed a double full-stop (..), which must be corrected. This, on a programme whose sole aim was to improve communications and situational awareness, reducing casualties. (You might well ask why he was employed).

This example exposes many of the day-to-day obstacles placed in the way of MoD's procurers - by their own management. It also partly explains the criticism by the Defence Committee in 2010 when noting 3,900 (11%) BOWMAN radios had gone 'missing'. The following year this was updated to 5,961, worth £184M. (The committee was inconsistent with its valuations, this being at the lower end of its various estimates, and it didn't specify which radios). MoD at first said they had not been counted because they were being repaired or had been redeployed; later claiming it had no proper accounting system. The system was excellent, it just wasn't used. While correctly blaming this poor accounting, the committee omitted that many users didn't even open the BOWMAN box, as they'd been using more modern and better kit for a decade.

At a January 2006 press briefing, the Capability Manager for Battlefield Manoeuvre, a General, called VISIGOTH *'The comms system of choice in Afghanistan'*. Another swipe at BOWMAN. Nobody asked why there was a choice. VISIGOTH had already delivered the best solution. BOWMAN was delivering something two generations older that the Infantry didn't want. And a third project had specified something the Infantry couldn't use even if it wanted to. And then matters got considerably worse...

Flaming hell

Power, in general, is termed a 'critical enabling technology', for obvious reasons. For example, the above briefing revealed that by 2006 most Special Forces missions in Afghanistan were being terminated due to a lack of battery power, rather than operational reasons.

In military applications the environment is a crucial consideration. Batteries must be charged in both extreme heat and cold. The colder it is the less the charge current must be, as the cells will overheat, so temperature compensation is required. Overheating will eventually lead to fire, but less obviously the heat signature can be detected by the enemy. When a battery is recharged it will not go back to full charge, and capacity is reduced. Typically, one seeks 500 recharging cycles to 80% of the original charge. If a battery is exhausted, safety circuitry kicks in to safeguard its cells; so, the charger will indicate a fault condition and reject it. A commercial charger is unsuitable.

It was not that MoD didn't understand this. It did, and had superb experts. But they were not engaged, BOWMAN was insular, and their cells, batteries and chargers did not perform as an integrated system. The cells were made by a sub-contractor and assembled by the battery contractor, under contract to the BOWMAN prime contractor, General Dynamics. The batteries failed after only a few attempts at charging, and could not be recovered from deep discharge; despite the manufacturers claiming over 1,000 charging cycles. Of note, the battery supplier didn't have the necessary MoD accreditations. The situation became intolerable when, shortly after delivery, BOWMAN Lithium-Ion batteries were the subject of a recall and destruction order, due to what MoD euphemistically called *'flaming events'*.

Replacement began the following year. At the time, BOWMAN had procured around 73,000 batteries, with a further 42,000 to come; at a total cost of around £35M (2006 prices, and roughly 30% of MoD's total buy). The shortage was forcing the MoD project team to consider a further buy of 100,000. The major difficulty they faced, apart from complaints from front line, was that battery replenishment funding was based on a life of 500 cycles. Plainly, if the battery died after 5 charges, funding had to increase and be immediately available. A complication was that BOWMAN's batteries for UHF, VHF and HF radios were not interchangeable; to an extent unavoidable if one chooses to buy separate radios, but one must make adequate compensatory provision. One interim measure was to procure a single HF/VHF/UHF radio under an Urgent Operational Requirement. The users were ecstatic, especially as its battery actually worked; and were reluctant to give them up, regarding BOWMAN as a downgrade.

Other project offices had long regarded this recall inevitable, predicting what would happen in precise and gory detail. It critically depleted battery supplies at a time when military demands had the world's factories at full capacity. When a Freedom of Information request was submitted in August 2006, a Brigadier replied confirming all this.[24] Worse, the same supplier was used for the replacements, when other UK-based suppliers had proven systems at a fraction of the price...

Power mad

At the same time, a requirement was being put out to tender by the Dismounted Close Combat team (DCC) to develop a Portable Power System for infantrymen. Bidders were to propose a method of maturing existing technologies, in a word-capped submission. There were many

---

24 Letter BLD/3/10, 5 September 2006. BOWMAN battery recall.

possibilities (batteries, fuel cells, hybrids, micro-generators, etc.), using many chemistries. The cap meant each could be addressed only in broad terms.[25]

However, one supplier (as above) was given access to a 2004 Defence Scientific Advisory Council (DSAC) report, setting out MoD's preferred solution. (The DSAC reports directly to the Secretary of State for Defence). Moreover, they were given briefings by DCC. The report even lists the attendees.[26] When other bidders asked for a copy, DCC refused. So too DSAC.[27] The advantage was clear, and a 3-year Research and Development contract was awarded, to deliver one phase per year.

This, despite another bidder, used by other parts of MoD, undertaking to satisfy Phase 1 with an off-the-shelf product, not the technical paper or prototype requested by DCC; the company noting that 17,000 of these systems were already in use by the British Army. Its Phase 2 proposal would be an upgrade to this legacy system, with delivery imminent. Phase 3, a hybrid solution and also under development, would be delivered within one year. The company added that Phases 1 and 2 would resolve the aforementioned BOWMAN charging problem.

How did scrutiny miss that 17,000 systems were already in service that met the specification? *(Step #7)*.

So, DCC chose to ignore a bid from a reputable supplier, promising a faster, cheaper and better capability, in favour of one who had already failed miserably. These were the three strands of the 'Smart Acquisition' initiative, introduced as part of the Strategic Defence Review of 1998. Senior approval would be needed to ignore such a bid. Hansard is revealing, offering clues such as favourable parliamentary statements and, later, an Executive Directorship for a former Defence Minister.

This losing bidder also notified the DCC contracts manager their bid would realise savings of over £100M if MoD would consider using the same working voltage across several equipment programmes. They had spotted that Portable Power System, BOWMAN, and Future Integrated Soldier Technology (FIST) specified different voltages. (15/24, 14.4 and 7.2 respectively). This was particularly inept, as DCC also managed FIST.

---

25 Invitation to Tender CA/C/00072. Portable Power System.
26 Report D/DSAC/65/2, 4 March 2004. 'Portable Power Systems and Energy Storage for Future Soldier and similar Land Battle Technology'.
27 Letter D/CST/06/01/10/04, 17 November 2005.

The contracts manager didn't reply.

On 4 April 2006 the company submitted a letter of appeal to the Defence Procurement Agency's Commercial Director, a 2-Star. It was copied to the Defence Procurement Minister, Lord Drayson, and listed a number of breaches of the Commercial Codes of Practice.[28] Of the seven Codes relating to the tendering phase, DCC breached six. The seventh was not applicable to this tender. The appeal was rejected.

Enjoying this top level support, the contracts manager continued to refuse to meet the company, merely offering a written reply containing a series of easily disproved claims. Actually, lies. Chief among them, that the Invitation to Tender did not link the requirement to BOWMAN or FIST, causing her to mark down the company's bid.[29] In fact, it said:

'The programme shall address the requirements for interfacing the portable power systems with other power consuming systems, including connectivity, power control circuits, etc. for FIST, BOWMAN and Special Projects systems'.

They had also been marked down for assuming use of the Royal School of Signals at Blandford during trials, despite DCC requiring:

'The planning and execution of troop trials at the Infantry Trials and Development Unit, Warminster and/or at the Royal School of Signals, Blandford, of the prototype Portable Power'.

Moreover, her tender assessment scheme allocated 20 of 100 available marks to agreeing Terms & Conditions and Intellectual Property Rights - mostly statements of fact and acceptance. But only one to safety - at a time when troops were being injured and killed due to defective and unsafe batteries.[30] Of the 30 distinct components of the assessment, the non-favoured bidders were disadvantaged in 17 due to her refusal to establish a level playing field. Someone who does this, and insists their staff to do likewise, is likely to be an habitual offender. Not only was the waste astronomical, this is almost identical to the Nimrod ANR case discussed earlier. At least there was a consistency.

One of MoD's power specialists at the time, who had been excluded from the process, predicted:

'Portable Power System will be allowed to run for two years to save face, and

---

28 MoD/Industry Commercial Policy Group, Guideline Number 5. 'Defence Acquisition - The Commercial Framework, Best Codes of Practice', September 2001.
29 DPA letter CA/A/00072, 6 April 2006.
30 CA/A/00072 Marking Scheme, 28 October 2005.

then cancelled'.
The selected contractor failed to deliver and it was cancelled.

Interestingly, BOWMAN knew <u>nothing</u> of Portable Power System. When told, the team leader confirmed that the performance of the off-the-shelf system far exceeded that of the one they had; especially in the critical areas of temperature range and life cycle. He also admitted a serious shortfall of AC chargers, and a huge backlog of discharged batteries; Hullavington Barracks (9 Logistics Squadron) being forced to park Land Rovers outside the barracks with engines running all night, using the DC chargers to attempt to recover the batteries. The problem he faced was that MoD's policy was 'hands off sub-contractors'. He could only encourage the losing bidder to speak to General Dynamics; who were polite, but said no, they would stick with the failed supplier.

This policy of focussing on prime contractors, to the exclusion of sub-contractors (who usually account for about 70% of the total cost) is counter-productive. If a problem arose with a sub, as it did here and placing the entire project (not to mention lives) at risk, MoD wasn't interested, telling the prime *'That's your problem'*. This is the worst kind of abrogation, and the admission by the team leader should have been accompanied by a head-banging session whereby the prime was told to use a supplier who could actually deliver what MoD asked for.

A further problem with this policy is that MoD has little visibility of progress. Its aim, to transfer as much risk as possible to the prime, ignores that industry's resources are not infinite, and they can't be expected to absorb all risk. The mitigation is to *avoid the avoidable, manage the unavoidable*. Here, the decision to continue with a favoured supplier, in the face of huge losses and waste, was entirely avoidable.

This all sounds like doom and gloom, but there were positives. Future Business Group, who provided the funding, were incandescent over the DCC contract manager's performance; who, of course, blamed her staff despite her name being all over the correspondence. And unfortunately for DCC, the Group leader's brother-in-law was Lord Drayson, who took it upon himself to visit and get it first-hand.

The way MoD works is that it would never admit this, but behind the scenes changes quietly took place. It was conceded that DCC had no grasp of what Portable Power System meant, or its links to FIST and

BOWMAN; but by then the contracts manager was up and away. Where was the project manager in all this? A scientist, while he sat in DCC he was not part of the team, and had been largely ignored.

The most serious violations were briefing only one company during the DSAC's work, and then claiming to other bidders there was no relationship between its report and the requirement. That was maladministration, and the Commercial Director approved it.

I should say here that the appalling behaviour of the contracts manager is a rarity. I worked with scores of superb contracts officers, most of whom would cringe at what I've related. I should perhaps also assure you I have never worked for any of the bidders, nor did I ever have any under contract. However, in 2002 I was asked to give a presentation on systems integration to the DCC team, including the same contracts manager. They insisted that the very concept of Safety Cases for weapons, propellants and explosives was *'a complete waste of money'*. These are the type of people who bring a financier to a safety meeting.

An aside

The battery issue (above) was a root cause of the Boeing 787 Dreamliner Lithium-Ion battery *'flaming events'* (actually, near catastrophic fires) in 2013-14, grounding the aircraft. (Intriguingly, Boeing used the same term as MoD eight years before). The line taken by Boeing and the Federal Aviation Administration (FAA) was that it was okay to vent fumes/smoke, but not have flames. The trouble is, if the electrolyte is venting that means there is already a fire within the cell. Boeing's 'solution' was to contain the fire within in a huge stainless steel box. Most aircraft engineers, aircrew and passengers would prefer there to be no fire in the first place.

While heads were being scratched in Boeing and the FAA, the similar Airbus A350 system had a correct design. That being so, inevitably the question of *savings at the expense of safety* arises.

Group 2 - Finance

10. *Is it sensible in relation to the Defence Programme?*
11. *Is it sensible in relation to the Service's Programme as a whole?*
12. *Is it sensible in relation to the Service's Equipment Programme?*
13. *Is there adequate provision? If so, given the other priorities, should it retain its place in the Programme? Does some current economy proposal cast doubt over the proposal?*
14. *If the provision is inadequate or the requirement is a new one, might room be found in the Programme? i.e. what offsets can be found?*
15. *Are there any acceptable changes in the requirement which could reduce the cost?*
16. *Is the size of the proposed contractual commitment commensurate with the nature of the requirement and its priority within the Programme?*
17. *Does the estimate contain all the associated costs; e.g. aircraft integration costs?*
18. *Have the industrial and technical risks been identified and costed?*
19. *Is it covered by a NATO Infrastructure category? If so, what has been done to obtain NATO approval? Is the degree of NATO approval sufficient to minimise the risk to Defence funds?*

While headed 'Finance', once again most questions fall within the Provisioning Authority's remit, with Financial & Secretariat advising on offsets and underspends. The project office will assist with #18; and #19 will usually have been answered when approving the basic requirement. #17 is where scrutiny frequently breaks down, failing to ensure an item of equipment perform within the wider system, and is functionally safe. (See BOWMAN battery/charger case).

Balls of crystal

In 1990 Air Member Supply and Organisation (AMSO) introduced two profligate policies related to avionic repair contracts.

First, they demanded that all contracts be Firm Price. Hitherto, one might send an item in for repair. The company would diagnose the fault at an agreed *fixed* price, and give MoD a quote for repair at a *fixed* hourly rate, *plus* the cost of materiel. This was controlled via the Local Equipment Repair Committee (LERC), chaired by the project manager. The subtlety here is that the minutes of a LERC are immediately contractually binding, and contracts branch are not involved. The flexibility this provided was one of MoD's best efficiency tools.

But now the companies had to provide a price, sight unseen. They pointedly replied: *'What's going to be wrong with it?'*. One cannot predict this on avionics, where the kit is allowed to fail, and those failures are random. Whereas, if asked to cost the overhaul of a gearbox, it is basically serviceable when returned and the same 100% replacement spares are required each time, such as bearings, seals and locking devices. Nasty surprises are minimal.

An example - Lynx and Sea Harrier radar Transmitters. The most expensive component was the (common) spin-tuned magnetron. Ferranti would now have to assume *every* Transmitter would need a new magnetron. If they didn't, they would make a huge loss. Either way, the RN would have to wait longer and face even bigger shortages, because one couldn't just buy one magnetron - the manufacturer simply wouldn't accept such an order. Unserviceable Transmitters would have to accumulate until an economic production run was needed.

Production yield is key, with most of the failures early in the process; so a larger production run costs less per unit, meaning it is cheaper to order more than strictly needed. Often, these very expensive items would be held at companies, not MoD stores depots, because they had to be 'exercised' to maintain their performance. Service demands would be forwarded to the company, who would be paid a small handling fee to distribute them. All this was completely invisible to front line. This ceased. Ostensibly serviceable equipment would be delivered from depots to front line and not work, because it had not been maintained.

Meanwhile, the 'system' would say more Transmitters had to be bought. But this would fail scrutiny because they weren't required - the solution being to revert to previous practice. But AMSO insisted, as *Firm Price* got them a nice tick in their box. The fact that it cost at least twice as much, and front line went without, was, to them, irrelevant.

Now, if you will, multiply this across hundreds of avionic systems. Where was the money to come from? Nobody in AMSO knew, or had even thought of it, because once again the proposed policy had not been circulated for comment or scrutiny.

The waste was immediate, vast, and chronic. Aircraft were soon flying around with yawning gaps in their equipment racks; later confirmed under oath by Flight Lieutenant Iain MacFarlane at the 1996 Fatal Accident Inquiry into the loss of 29 passengers and aircrew in Chinook ZD576. He remains the RAF's most decorated pilot, and stated Chinooks were even lacking windows and flight instruments. AMSO told the squadrons it was another procurement cock-up. No. The procurers were the only ones who did their duty. But had that been all, it might have been manageable...

Second, AMSO applied a 'repair calculation'. Hitherto, equipment fed-in for repair was on an *as required* basis, the aim being to maintain minimum stock levels, plus Contingency and War Reserves. This required Buffer Stock to be held, but it had been scrapped under DM87.

The system relies on the Provisioning Authority getting his Capital Buy quantities (i.e. main equipment) right first time, within acceptable margins, and keeping it so. Due to attrition (e.g. damaged equipment being uneconomical to repair) he seldom has too much, so it is usually a case of ensuring everything unserviceable is in the repair loop. Only when a fleet size is reduced or a type leaves service will surpluses be generated (although if sold on to another country, quite often a shortage is created by having to provide them with our spares). This sounds complex but is relatively straight-forward, the key being to know what you have. (But see BOWMAN - MoD doesn't).

But now, AMSO (they claimed) would at the beginning of the financial year declare how many units would fail in the following 12 months, why, and the precise cost of repair. That sum would be set aside, and not a penny more. In which font of wisdom did they dip this wet finger? Only they knew, and weren't saying, despite their own regulations requiring them to give five months' notice of the proposed contract details, and justification, to the Service Engineering Authority.[31] Bad enough, but they excluded War Reserves, loans and trials equipment. This equipment, that the government decrees must be held at immediate readiness, was to lie unserviceable and, in many cases, scrapped.

A good example of this arose whenever RAF Harriers had to deploy on carriers. For safety reasons they had to be fitted with an RN equipment, the I-Band Transponder. When illuminated by the ship's primary radar,

---

31 AP830 DG9/1, Part 2, Para 7b(1).

the transponder replies with an enhanced, coded signal, identifying it as 'friendly' at a glance. Shelf stock had to be exercised every six months, and the frequency of the magnetron checked to ensure drift was not excessive. Now they would not be. Also, it can be seen that usage was not constant, surging every time the RAF deployed. This required significant stock to be available at short notice, rendered the 'repair calculation' false. (It didn't help that the RAF usually 'forgot' to return the loaned kit, yet never seemed to have any by the next deployment).

More fundamentally, the repair contract is an MoD contract, not the suppliers'. It is used by other departments - project office, Technical Agency, Quality Assurance and the Services - for matters which supply branches need not be aware of. Their new policy overlooked this. There could only be one outcome. Rampant waste. But this mattered not to AMSO, as the funding they now said would be necessary was lower than MoD(PE) had used, which they presented as an 'efficiency'. That it would produce nothing tangible was ignored. Told not to expect as much work, companies had to let people go. Trust was lost.

All this exacerbated the effect of DM87, which had already caused funding to run out less than three months into the financial year. Now, even more front line demands couldn't be met. Shortly, the repair calculation on every contract had to be increased. Companies had to recruit again, and train new staff. Their overhead rates (dictated by MoD) shot up. This ill-conceived policy cost the Services dear in a period dominated by the first Gulf War. Post-action reports would flow down saying *We were short of this...* Conveniently, AMSO were tasked with responding.

In September 1990, having been fobbed off by suppliers, and after consulting with the project manager, the RAF Main Building office responsible for Nimrod R1 (Sigs 5) wrote to their supply branch managing the aircraft's Electronic Intelligence equipment:

'The inflexible repair contracts are causing supply problems due to delays in obtaining contract amendments. Op GRANBY is exacerbating the problems of supply due to higher levels of aircraft utilisation. The problems can be minimised by letting contracts "as required". There are no surplus LRUs or modules and therefore we need to have all equipment repaired as it becomes unserviceable. An "as required" contract will not result in equipment being repaired unnecessarily. Sensible levels of Requirement Approval can be given

based on previous spend, which will not compromise LTC provision.[32]

AMSO(RAF) turned their back on... the RAF. Luckily, there being few RIs, the problem was able to be managed locally, with the likes of Hewlett-Packard only too happy to help RAF Wyton's Special Role Bay and Electronic Warfare and Avionic Detachment, whose roles were to support 51 Squadron. (They were the jewels in the RAF support crown). Costs were charged to whatever contract happened to be available. Strictly speaking prohibited, but with the chain of command in this extraordinary period being Cabinet Office > Sigs 5 > project manager, the latter probably felt secure. (More of R1 in Group 4).

Other front line aircraft didn't fare so well. Two years later, in September 1992, RAF Hercules fleet managers were still making identical complaints, unable to get stocks of the Cloud and Collision Warning Radar mentioned earlier. It was only with these ever more desperate pleas that junior supply managers (Squadron Leader level) acknowledged the problem. They escalated the matter, and over the next few years matters improved to a degree - in that the pain was spread more evenly. The only real change was the argument was now taking place in the correct corridors; but making the cover-up easier.

To the begging we will go

A 'Form 9' is a Request for Additional Financial Cover. It is what it says. If additional funding is required over and above the endorsed amount, for any reason, a Form 9 is raised by the project manager on the finance office. They most often apply to In Service Support.

To recap, the project manager is the one with Technical and Financial Approval. He must seek the customer's agreement the work is still required, and in signing the Form 9 he is saying the new, higher cost is *'fair and reasonable'*. The financier does not approve the increase. He says if it's available, or if an underspend or offset can be used.

A major reason for Form 9s was that the RAF supply computer would be populated with cost data gleaned from the original production contract. Naturally, this figure became increasingly out-of-date, most obviously due to inflation. But that didn't matter as the price would be updated if a new buy became necessary, and only then would funding

---

32 D/DSS(Air)35/19/2, 12 September 1990. 'Nimrod R1 Role Equipment Repair Policy'.

approval be sought. That is, the Provisioning Authority would:

a) Identify requirement,

b) Establish cost,

c) Confirm funding and approve or seek approval,

d) Send it to the project manager, to procure.

But when AMSO took over management of all air stores and the budget, and with Provisioning Authorities done away with, no proper scrutiny was possible. They would:

a) Not verify the 'requirement' or subject it to scrutiny,

b) Approve funding based on the original cost,

c) Send it to the project manager, bypassing the user, who would establish true cost and raise a Form 9.

The customer had no input, even to say if they actually needed the kit. *(Step #1)*. If he agreed with the requirement, the project manager had to raise a Form 9 for the deficit; whereas before this would be rare.

It can be seen the headache this caused; and remember, this was happening across <u>all</u> avionics. The correct cost was only established far too late in the day. If the RAF could not find the shortfall, the contract would have to be suspended, cancelled, or numbers cut. (In turn increasing unit cost again). In time this became the norm, the RN complaining to AMSO:

'Having funded a Fit Policy, the RN is now in the unique position of being prevented from implementing it by a series of new financial rules applied by persons either disinterested or inexperienced in the RN's modus operandi.'[33]

Specifically, they were referring to supporting aircraft embarked at sea for six months, a concept the RAF system couldn't cope with. *Their* worst nightmare was something going unserviceable in Hong Kong or Cyprus, the spare being put on the next flight out of RAF Lyneham or Brize Norton. This led to some bizarre exchanges.

HMS Ark Royal, steaming towards Sydney to participate in the Australian bi-centennial celebrations, reported a Transmitter/Receiver had failed, which they couldn't repair. They had spares onboard - it was

---

33 Director General Aircraft (Navy) response to letter DDSM(AV)11(RAF) 2/10/1, 28 January 1992.

a routine heads-up to suppliers of what to expect for repair upon return to the UK; and for their next storing demand (coordinated by a different Supply Branch). That is, storing a ship prior to deployment is a huge surge on the system, and to be forewarned is to be prepared.

But AMSO's good book told them to send a spare to Lyneham or Brize, saying *'Fly it to Ark Royal'*. Not knowing what to do, or where Ark was, or how to find out, this quickly landed on a Navy desk in London. Told of the reality, supply managers insisted on it being delivered. Asked how they proposed to do this, they replied *'It's an aircraft carrier, we'll land onboard'*. Told a Hercules or VC10 couldn't land on an Invincible Class carrier: *'We'll airdrop it'*. (It weighed 55lbs, plus packing, and would need flotation kit). But Hong Kong to Sydney is almost 5,000 miles by sea. A quick look at their instructions. *'We'll arrange refuelling'*. And so on.

I'm afraid the RN chap had a field day, and quite possibly a hernia; but the serious aspect is that the RN had been instructed to transfer their entire air stores inventory and its funding to the RAF for management, without any form of scrutiny to determine if they could actually do the job; aggravated by the ancient RAF computer system being unable to 'see' ships. (The RN one, which was more modern and specifically programmed for their unique needs, fell into disuse). The RAF's position was they'd delivered the kit to RNAS Culdrose in Cornwall. That the squadron then embarked on Ark Royal and was on the other side of the world was invisible to them. They would say to Culdrose training and Search and Rescue squadrons, the simulator, workshops and Tactical Analysis Centre: *You're not getting* (your) *kit because you already have some*. At first the RN shook their head, thinking: *They'll learn*. But when a young supplier demands of a senior RN officer: *Under what authority did you remove the kit from Culdrose and take it to Australia?*, you know you're in deep, long-term trouble.

While the RN knew what their budget *should* be, they were concerned it was being used up at the beginning of the financial year. Where was it going? They weren't seeing any return. The answer soon became apparent - AMSO was initially allocating it to RAF requirements, leaving crumbs. *First come, first served*, regardless of priority, ownership, or the actual endorsed requirement; and the RN had no presence at Harrogate so weren't in any queue. In the same exchange (above), the RN characterised their 'Customer/Supplier' relationship as *'Beggar/Supplier'*.

It is difficult to overstate how big a shock this was to the RN. There is always inter-Service rivalry and banter, but there is also mutual respect and support. If there was something to be said at this level, the RN would send in their civilian engineers. Their Admirals would stand 4-square behind them, leaving junior officers out of it. But AMSO's actions brought utter fury, and soon RN officers (and indeed RAF engineering officers) of all ranks were openly hostile towards these new policies. This was particularly disturbing for the vast majority of suppliers, who were invariably quite young ladies. They looked to the more mature (who perhaps had had a career break to raise a family - *am I allowed to say such a thing today?*), or the more outspoken, to speak on their behalf. *They* were given short shrift, and there quickly came a time when they sought help from the older project managers in London. But there is no real mechanism to deal with this. Civilian Personnel departments won't listen to concerns about a serving officer. *'They can do what they want';* even if that breaches every known Personnel regulation. (Personnel are not your friend. They exist only to indemnify the Executive Board).

At the working level, the obstructions were initially and primarily at junior (Wing Commander and Squadron Leader) level in the RN-peculiar Supply Branch (SM47); in time overflowing into those managing RAF and common equipment. Did these RAF officers resent being given RN work? Was it was perhaps a form of punishment posting? When challenged, they knew precisely what the effects of their actions were, openly inviting the RN to take a hike. Their Group Captain did <u>not</u> support them, but everyone above him did, leaving him ostracised along with the project managers.

This exchange arose from a minor issue, the final straw being a handwritten note to a project manager from said Wing Commander. His staff had sent some Radio Altimeters to Plessey for repair. This was over and above the repair calculation, so there was a shortfall in funding. The previous project office, in MoD(PE), had raised a Form 9 but SM47 had not replied. Plessey had completed the repairs on trust.

The work had then transferred to a project office in AMSO, under the same Air Commodore as the suppliers. The new <u>RAF</u> project manager, facing a demand from Plessey that invoices be paid, raised a duplicate Form 9 on the <u>same</u> finance office, noting the previous attempt.

But the Wing Commander had instructed them to forward any Form 9 requests for his personal scrutiny and, it transpired, automatic rejection. Not only were AMSO staff at loggerheads with the RN and RAF engineers, and front line, they were now arguing amongst themselves.

79

The note said:

'The attached F9 is returned unactioned. There is something wrong with the initial contract if we are forever seeking additional funds. I cannot and will not run my budget this way'.

A few things will be apparent. A supply officer had been granted (or assumed) Technical and Financial Approval for 'his' budget, when the legitimate delegation sat with the project manager. More to the point, *his* supply staff had structured the *'initial contract'*, stating a maximum quantity to be fed-in for repair. They had exceeded this quantity without confirming it could be paid for. The reason why the project managers were *'forever seeking additional funds'* was because AMSO had actively sought to bypass their role, and were ignoring the regulations.

The project managers were accused of incompetence for allowing contractors to rip MoD off with inflated prices. Most chose to move on, their view of AMSO forever tainted. I cannot say what the cumulative waste was. The budget was finite, but AMSO were now <u>committing funding they didn't have</u>.

I chose these Altimeter and Transponder examples because they were managed in quite separate Navigation and Radar Directorates; but there are hundreds of avionic systems, most more complex and costly. On a big-ticket one can look at the endorsement and bills paid, and calculate the difference. But here there were thousands of contracts, spread across many Directorates. The true waste was incalculable, and <u>recurring</u>.

When the next (il)logical step was taken - privatising 3rd Line workshops and 2nd Line support at Air Stations - the financial baseline used in any Investment Appraisal was entirely false. MoD might be spending £2M a year maintaining a given equipment. A company might quote £1.9M, and it would be spun as £100k savings. But this ignored that until recently it was all done for half the price and twice as quickly. Everyone knew this; industry, MoD HQs, project offices - and AMSO.

But one cannot be wrong by virtue of one's rank. Those who knew the truth were shut down. In fact, threatened. Many companies complained bitterly. They knew that if MoD wastes its money reputations suffer. Motive within MoD? Personal gain - kudos for alleged 'savings', and advancement.

I know what MoD will say. *We contract most of this out now, so no longer a problem.* Wrong. It's still a problem, because the root cause remains.

Failure to conduct Requirement Scrutiny. When one has a personal duty, abrogation is not delegation.

You haven't done the work? That's okay, submit your bill.

After placing a contract, payment is the most visible method of rewarding satisfactory progress. Payment milestones must be carefully negotiated by the project manager (not contracts branch), and must be satisfactory deliverables which will benefit MoD.

On a Development contract (the most difficult in this sense) the best starting point is Configuration Milestones, such as Preliminary Design Review and Critical Design Review. These are presentations by the company to the project manager, offering evidence that the work has been successfully completed. As the project progresses the evidence moves from plans and specifications, to drawings, to testing and trialling prototypes; and, clearly, the project manager must be able to interpret this evidence. Sometimes the Review is formal, sometimes stand-up meetings at integration rigs, and then in the trials aircraft. And on one notable occasion in a Virgin Atlantic flight to Florida, who were most upset when a company engineer produced a bag of tools. The kit didn't work at take-off, but did upon landing, and the trials at the Atlantic Underwater Trials and Evaluation Centre were successful.

This anecdote has a point. Try booking a nuclear submarine for sonics trials. They give you a date three years hence, and you <u>must</u> hit it. It's seldom if ever missed, which should generate questions as to how. I've been there. The trials helicopter hovering in the dip in the Western Isles, and the submarine's conning tower magically appeared bang on time. And the kit in the helicopter (and hanging from it) <u>had</u> to work, as the sub disappeared again and went on its way. Five minutes late? Tough, the Captain ain't turning round. No second chances. No contract extensions. No final payment. To some projects, being on time is a given. 'Late' is not in their vocabulary. Those who manage these things need to be listened to.

The approach MoD takes with industry, hands-on or off, depends largely on the nature of the work. Official guidance is hands-off by default, but in practice the project manager and Quality Assurance Officers will have been constantly checking progress, often getting involved in the design, and the Review(s) should be a final check in the presence of the Service. The primary aim is to establish a baseline for the next phase. That is, if anything goes wrong one need (contractually) only regress one step. Of course, it would be naïve to think this works every time, but it is a good foundation.

The project manager is permitted, within his delegated powers, to make a partial (or discretionary) payment if the milestone criteria has not been met; say, because an MoD dependency has not been delivered. But he is forbidden from making payment if, all other things being equal, the work has not been carried out successfully or satisfactorily. This rather assumes he has Technical and Financial Approval delegation. But in the mid/late-90s the number of non-technical project managers was increasing. Not a huge problem, so long as the correct person was managing the milestones. But, these non-engineers were permitted to self-delegate Technical and Financial Approval. Warned as to the illegality of their actions, some simply carried on.

This was taken to a lethal extreme on the Sea King ASaC Mk7 *programme*. The non-technical *project* manager for the Mission System Upgrade waived the Critical Design Review for the aircraft installation design, a part of the *programme* he had no involvement in. This was the final defence in depth that would have *emphasised* the risks associated with the contributory factors later noted in the 2003 accident. A written declaration was required confirming the Review was successful. It was false. Motive was clear. He had cancelled the risk mitigation work, knowing this left the aircraft vulnerable to mid-air collision. On 4 June 1998 his subordinate, the *programme* manager, wrote pointing out concerns that he, Boscombe Down and the RN had over safety arising from this fraud, finishing:

> '*To not even insist on a Critical Design Review when the main subject is electrical and structural integrity of the aircraft is beyond me'.*[34]

Safe in the comfort of top level support, he did not reply.

Plumbing the depths

A project manager was investigating a case of suspected fraud. This related to two contracts to upgrade Active Dipping Sonar equipment, part of a 'deep water' enhancement package. Ludicrously, Director General Underwater Weapons (DGUW) had been charged with

---

34 D/DHP/71/1/5/2, 4 June 1998.

managing the winch and Submersible Unit upgrades; the aircraft office the Pithead Gear and avionics upgrades, and buying the new cable. The DGUW files had been transferred to the aircraft office after (alleged) completion, and all monies being paid, so all records would now be held in one location. The respective project managers were long gone.

Almost immediately, Bill Paying Branch in Liverpool asked the new Sea King avionics manager to approve further expenditure of over £1M on DGUW's contracts; DGUW having washed their hands of it by virtue of the transfer. He refused, investigated, and uncovered fifteen instances of double-billing, one of triple-billing, five of claiming and receiving payment for work not carried out, and five lost winches; over a five-year period. He submitted a report to his Assistant Director.[35]

MoD's auditors ruled it an administrative error. Director of Helicopter Projects raged. The company was merely required to issue credit notes against future contracts, meaning there would be no guarantee *his* aircraft funding would benefit. And it didn't. Nevertheless, this showed the benefits of a project manager actually knowing something about kit that wasn't in his current remit, and being able to conduct scrutiny.

Grub's up

All project managers know about the world and its dog pitching up at meetings, but having little or no role. Attendance is at his discretion, but he has no authority over other departments, who can just ignore him. In time my boss, Ray, got utterly fed up with this, and demanded a complete cull. Still they rolled up.

Matters came to a head one day when a serving officer arrived at a factory in West Sussex, with a Senior NCO as his driver. When asked why two of them were there, when neither was required, he replied that he had heard the company served a good wine at lunchtime and intended getting sloshed at 'their' expense.

I postponed the meeting for half an hour and called the Contracts and Catering Managers together for a chat. I told them that, henceforth, lunch would be sandwiches, not a 3-course meal, and no alcohol. The Catering Manager wasn't happy but understood, and their senior management were content because I gave an assurance the money saved would pay for a much needed software engineer. The contract value

---

35 Letter report D/DHP 48/5/7, 7 November 1994.

wouldn't change.

Ray was pleased, but it didn't make too much difference to him as they didn't serve Dim Sum. He preferred the company coming to London and lunch in Chinatown. The privilege of rank, and being such a good radar engineer they liked to pick his brains.

This doesn't sound much, but bear in mind MoD had thousands of contracts with hundreds of contractors, on avionics alone. For whatever reason, MoD attendance went from double figures to at most three, and matters became far more efficient. Front line suddenly noticed software tasks were being delivered in weeks rather than months or even years. *Look after the pennies...*

Another side of the coin

MoD's rules on detached duty travel say to use the most economical means. An elderly engineer in the Aircraft Support Executive (Navy) at Yeovilton was told by his civilian line manager to hitch it to Ferranti in Edinburgh, about 430 miles. He did, carrying classified files he needed for the visit.

Around the same time, a 16-year old admin assistant from London was attending a training course at Kentigern House, Glasgow. MoD booked the cheapest hotel it could find. She arrived at midnight to find it was an hourly rate... Her dad went ballistic. Wouldn't you?

Group 3 - Manpower

20. Have the manpower implications been identified?

21. Is any manpower saving a real saving or will it merely reduce 'overstretch'?

22. If these are any additional manpower requirements, have the sources from which those will be met been clearly identified?

Responsibility for bidding for the correct manpower initially rests with the Directorates of Equipment Capability (DEC). Plainly, they need to take advice on project office manning. Today, this is an impossible area to get right, as a given level of expertise cannot be guaranteed. And the loss of one particular skill may force the work to be contracted out, at many times the cost. (The worst example I can recall is a programme manager who was allocated four hours per week in the Directorate Management Plan for one of his programmes. When it was transferred under a reorganisation, the new team successfully bid for four men to do the same task. And then had the audacity to ask for the job to be transferred back, as they didn't know what to do).

For industry, the project office will be aware of a company's capacity; and the act of bidding for and accepting a contract are statements that the correct resources and manpower are available and will be sustained.

The most serious manifestation can be seen in numerous accident reports where *lack of manpower* is a common theme. Equally as bad is *We have the manpower but they're not trained*. Three such high profile cases in recent years have been the deaths of Red Arrows pilot Sean Cunningham (2011) and Red Arrows engineer Jon Bayliss (2018), and the loss of a new F-35B Lightning off HMS Queen Elizabeth (2021). In each case the shortfalls had been identified, but the squadron and ship told to get on with it. The Defence Lines of Development process had simply recorded the requirement, not delivered it. This reflected MoD's long-standing approach to risk management; that it is sufficient to identify and record the risk. Mitigation is only considered if the risk materialises.

Now consider the roles of the top level committees. The Defence Board, Defence Audit and Risk Assurance Committee, and Executive Committee, each have 'risk' in their terms of reference. Specifically, the Defence Board is to *'ensure defence priorities and tasks are appropriately resourced'.* Responsibility is narrowed considerably. On F-35B one wouldn't expect DEC to say to Minister: *'We haven't enough engineers to check if the engine intake blanks have been removed before take-off'.* But they *are* required to tell him that the carrier design, and approval to commit to production, was predicated on a certain level of ship's company, and there is a critical shortfall causing increasing risk to life. And anyone rejecting a risk mitigation is <u>required</u> to place his reasoning in writing, not least because risk ownership transfers to him. Did senior officers dare notify the committees?

It's all about people

Upon being promoted into my first RN HQ job, my first task was to achieve a full fleet fit of surveillance radars in the Sea King HAS Mk5 fleet. There were 82 aircraft, only half were fitted, yet 126 equivalent systems had been bought and delivered. That is, equipment to the value of 126 systems, with fewer of the more reliable LRUs, and more of the less reliable ones. That didn't mean they were unreliable. They more than met their specification, but a Transmitter/Receiver (Tx/Rx) will always be less reliable than a Scanner.

The 'solution' on paper was to buy more systems, and £13M had been set aside. I was to apply engineering judgment before writing the Admiralty Board Submission. Given the newness of the radar I could not know its intricacies, although I was required to on a range of similar albeit older equipments. But having done the type of work you will know a man who does, usually the diagnostician on the 3rd Line repair bench - who it happened I'd trained. His shelves were creaking with Tx/Rx, each worth over £100k. I asked: *'What do you need?'*

1. A means of preventing corona discharge - High Tension (HT) cables in the Modulator Deck were arcing.

2. There were no spares of a particular printed circuit board.

Checking the Initial Spares Order contract from three years before, none of the boards had been bought. A simple clerical error and not worth mentioning. Quick call to the company for a price, tell Ranging and Scaling at Farnborough to update the Provisioning Data Slip, and get a buy under way. Delivered in a couple of months, for £25k.

Arcing... Slightly more complex. First, there had been a breakdown in the feedback and assessment process, the Design Authority unaware of the RN's concerns. Second, and the more immediate issue, the Tx/Rx sat under the floor in the aft avionics bay, positioned with its intake fan directly facing the bay's cooling intake. The drawback was, the engine efflux spewed at an angle down the airframe, and was sucked into the bay. This carbon deposit was going straight through the Tx/Rx's intake filter, and building-up on the HT leads; eventually causing severe arcing and damage. Just the other side of the transverse bulkhead? #4 and 5 Fuel Cells. Alarming, and a critical safety hazard.

Solution? Change the cooling convention in the bay? Expensive, but nevertheless had to be asked as newer Indian Sea Kings had the 'correct' arrangement. Also, one couldn't move the Tx/Rx, as it would impinge on its compass safe distance and lengthen the waveguide run to the Scanner. Simplest is often best. The HT leads were re-routed and an extra layer of heat-shrink sleeving applied; and a better filter specified, to be cleaned or changed more often. Not an onerous job as access to the bay was good, but still a maintenance burden on the squadrons. But rather that than onboard fires.

Occurrences ceased overnight, and full fleet fit was achieved in six months. Over £12.9M saved, reliability and availability improved, a pat on the back from the Admiral, Ron Holley, and a glass of sherry. But with hindsight my glasses were rose-tinted by his leadership. I soon learned that the vast majority of senior MoD staff took a dim view of anything that raised the bar of expectation. Later, in MoD(PE), the old hands would give me a look. *Been there, done it, got the scars.*

Experience not required

I mentioned the Suitably Qualified and Experienced Person (SQEP) principle; important when considering delegations; and ultimately the ability to deliver projects safely and successfully. This brings us to a little-known but destructive policy.

Project managers are only permitted to spend a maximum time in a post. The criteria was determined by the Directorate of Personnel, Resources and Development, but they were inconsistent. Sometimes it was time in a given Directorate. Sometimes time dealing with the same contractors. The period varied between 18 months and five years, the latter being (in theory) the absolute maximum. The constant was that one was no longer permitted to work with contractors with whom you'd had previous interaction. The perceived risk was fraud and corruption brought about by familiarity. One would simply receive a letter instructing you to start applying for other posts. No appeal was permitted, and Personnel were not required to explain their rationale. No notice need be given, and there was no time for succession planning.

The effect is devastating. Civilian line managers are reluctant to inform staff they have to move, because one can <u>always</u> point to many who don't have the policy applied to them - singling-out, which constitutes bullying and harassment. Cutting no ice with Personnel, who regard this as their entire *raison d'être*. The practical problem is that one must start again on annual reports, and work back up to (e.g.) a 'fitted for promotion' marking. To Personnel and management it is a weapon.

The one time I fell afoul of this, Personnel instructed my line manager, Colonel Barry Hodgkiss, to order me to move, on the grounds I had been *'in the same post for 18 months'*. Barry queried this, his concern being that the majority of his engineering staff had far more than 18 months in, and might have to go at a time when he needed all the expertise and experience he could muster. Personnel then changed the criteria to *'having been in the same or <u>related</u> appointment for five years'*. They confirmed 'related' meant anything connected with aviation, which I'd been doing for 25 years. So, I still had to go. A list of 261 companies was drawn up, essentially preventing me from working in Air Systems. Barry half-heartedly wrote to me advising me to start applying for jobs where I met the criteria - which would be very few. But he didn't press too hard, hoping Personnel would find something worthwhile to do.

Now, apply this to what else was going on; for example Nimrod MRA4 and Chinook HC Mk3. Did *they* suffer because of this misguided policy? Lack of SQEP is a common theme, and excuse, at Defence Committee hearings and in accident reports. So why get rid of them? Unsurprisingly, a question never asked at committee.

DICS picks

Project managers were required to attend training courses, but if they couldn't find a place within six months on-the-job training and experience gained was deemed sufficient. This worked well, as they already had many years' experience to draw on.

But lack of SQEP, and the intention that direct entrants become the majority, negated the training syllabi as the assumption of prior experience was no longer valid. To avoid highlighting this, MoD dumbed-down and all previous training was deemed not to have taken place. Everyone now had to attend new courses run by Portsmouth University. Staff who had successfully managed scores of projects were sent on Introduction to Project Management courses, where other attendees were new recruits yet to take up post.

The tutors realised their dilemma. At what level to pitch the course? Too low, and most would be bored in two minutes flat. Too high, and those who really needed to benefit would be lost in two minutes. They went low, and when it came to my turn the one week course was padded out with a final session on 'practical project management', a lecture to be given by a serving Colonel called Richard. *('Call me Dick')*.

Dick told us he was the project manager for something called 'Desert Integrated Computer System', which he had been allowed to name using the acronym DICS. The requirement was for two vehicles to be able to communicate with each other over a form of data link, using a computer in each. Pretty basic today, slightly more difficult then. Total cost, £500k. Eyebrows shot skywards. A Colonel with a single small project? MoD has a name for such jobs. 'Special Tasks', and they're given to junior staff to do in their spare time, often just for a bit of variety. Was the Army swimming in surplus Colonels?

Dick took us through the Acquisition Cycle so far. Project Initiation, Feasibility Studies, etc. Then he came to the procurement strategy, tendering and selection. Two bidders - simple you'd think, buy from the winner. But no. *'To avoid upset'*, he'd contracted one to each. I didn't quite catch the rest, as all 24 of us, plus tutors, were rolling in the aisles. This had to be a wind-up. So it still isn't clear to me if, say, one was a ZX Spectrum, the other an abacus. Either way, for some strange reason the system didn't work, with everyone blaming each other and no-one contracted to accept responsibility for the *integrated* system. (The clue is in the name). He was about to start again.

But here's the kicker. While MoD usually mans a project to cost, not content (a crucial flaw in its thinking, reflecting poor scrutiny and Lines of Development management), Dick had a full team. Technical Manager. Risk Manager. Quality Manager. Integrated Logistics Support Manager. We had whole aircraft programmes that didn't have any of these, and elsewhere in Air Systems Controllerate a Colonel was responsible for all Chinook and Lynx programmes.

We were convinced Dick had been set up. Or, perhaps, he'd been asked by an administrator who genuinely didn't see the conflict. After all, nowhere does MoD acknowledge that most projects are managed by individuals. The mantra is *'There's no "I" in Team'*. But that's all there is if you're a one-man band and no support to call upon.

Time was

Due to manpower cuts, a helicopter radar Maintenance Policy could no longer be implemented. A MoD(PE) project manager was asked if he would develop a new one. An easy enough job. Support of the radar stabilised. The savings were modest, a few million a year; and operational capability and effectiveness were enhanced, which one cannot put a price on. But what of the entire RN section, headed by a Commander, whose job this was? He had staff, but they weren't SQEP.

Why *that* project manager? A few years before, in 1989, he had noted these increasing shortcomings within Service HQs, proposing the formation of what he called an Integrated Project Team to oversee the stabilisation of Fire Control and Surveillance Radars, including Weather Radars. The team members were drawn from Service HQs, their Engineering Authorities, his own Finance and Contracts colleagues, and RAF supply managers. He was team leader, but not their line manager. *They* agreed that their staff would accept actions. Crucially, he had absolute control over the combined budgets, and could transfer money at will. Effectively, the aim of this MoD(PE)-led team was to ensure the Service HQ task was carried out; which probably wasn't easy to justify.

The team worked for over a year, meeting perhaps once a month and standing down when the situation was deemed stable. It could be said this was the forerunner of the Integrated Project Team model of 1999. The main differences in 1999 were: it was a permanent team and the team leader was line manager of most staff, but he didn't have the same flexibility with funding. Ask any team leader and he'll prefer the 1989 setup. His biggest headaches disappear.

Punch drunk

Future Integrated Soldier Technology (FIST) was a process, not a project. 'Future' - *yes, we're hoping to buy this*. 'Soldier' - *yes, that's who'll use it*. 'Technology' - *yes, that's what they'll use*. The key word was 'Integration'. Improved systems integration would increase operational tempo, get inside the enemy's decision cycle, and reduce casualties.

The challenges were:

- What technologies provided most benefit?
- Determine the point of diminishing returns.
- Provide justification, and seek approval to procure incrementally.
- Integrate to maximum benefit.

Integration and *Procurement* had to be separate. A basic principle applies. Integration development work is not volume-related. It must be done irrespective of numbers, and its funding ring-fenced and protected. But on FIST they were lumped together. The very act revealed (not for the first time) no cohesive understanding, either within DEC or the Investment Approvals Committee. This was, and remains, a recurring scrutiny failure, meaning no lessons are being learned. FIST had received approval to proceed, but its main component had not been defined. How did it pass scrutiny?

Boundary control would have to be established. That was the job of the Systems Integration Manager (SIM); whose position was a one-man team within a team. Quickly, 179 systems were identified that the soldier had to wear, carry, use or consume. These were grouped into the five Infantry domains (Lethality; Mobility; Survivability; Sustainability; Command, Control, Computing, Communications and Intelligence [C4I]), given defined Integration Levels, and prioritised. Five Levels were developed, the top one being:

'Complete *interoperable* functionality to include shared data environment. Full functionality and integration within FIST and with related equipment. All FIST and Non-FIST users have access to common data.'

The upshot was a Soldier System Integration and Interoperability Authority plan based on Defence Standard 05-125/2, mandated in all aviation contracts but setting out wider system integration principles and procedures. As Air Systems no longer used it, but had not issued any alternative, the SIM re-wrote the relevant chapters to cater for Soldier Systems. It was agreed with Defence Standards in Glasgow that he would issue and control it. The ripple effect of applying 05-125/2 on any project is unquantifiable and huge. It *forces* you to do the right thing.

The plan was approved, although 'Interoperability' removed because it is not policy for the Services to be interoperable with each other, never mind allies. A good attempt (he managed to retain it in the Integration Levels), but unfortunately spotted by Main Building. However, they didn't understand that retaining *interoperability* would have committed very little money, but would have enhanced corporate knowledge and made future Submissions easier. At a stroke, FIST was weakened to a dangerous degree. Perversely, some projects such as BOWMAN *did* include interoperability, so why exclude it from FIST when they had to be integrated? The inconsistency drives procurers up the wall.

However, while appointed Soldier Systems Integration Authority the SIM made an error by confining his plan to articulating how to *implement* system integration. The DCC Integrated Project Team Leader (sitting above the FIST team leader) didn't know what it was in the first place. Instead of simply asking the SIM to insert a few paragraphs, he let a 6-month contract on a consultant to *establish what integration was*. He and the contracts manager (see 'Power mad' in Group 1) approved this knowing it failed *Step #1*, as the SIM team demonstrably had the information. The consultant's report told the reader nothing about *implementation*. FIST regressed to *thinking* about integration.

A further hurdle popped up. MoD now had an Integration Authority; 63 civil servants headed by an externally recruited professor. Director General (Finance), to the SIM:

'We've discovered something called systems integration, and I've allocated £xxM over 3 years to establish what it all means'.

'You do know aircraft don't fly and ships don't sail without systems integration?'

Was this the level of thinking on the Defence Procurement Agency Executive Board? Perhaps they couldn't bring themselves to admit that elsewhere *implementing* integration was little more than a minor task for junior project officers, who would have been taught *what it means* as a 2nd year apprentice, and often *taught it* as a 4th year.

Meanwhile, the Integration Authority had offered no output, meaning few were aware of it. But the professor had been shown the SIM's plan by another recipient, and sought a meeting with the him and the FIST team leader. He had two issues:

- He was at pains to point out he was <u>MoD's</u> Integration Authority, not the Defence Procurement Agency's, which was simply where his office was. Therefore, the word 'Authority' must not be used by FIST, and <u>he</u> must sign and approve all plans.
- He would not sign them unless they were issued in *his* name, and *he* be allowed to take the credit for the SIM's work.

As FIST was, in effect, *Integration*, who was now in charge?

The discussion revealed he didn't know of 05-125/2, and presumably nor did his staff. But having been made aware, thereafter everything he did was reinventing a wheel. He, too, was willing to place the process (and soldiers) at risk for personal gain. Such empire builders cause huge problems, especially when they don't understand the difference between *Interface* and *Integration*, which the SIM had to explain to him. To the FIST team leader's annoyance, he had to agree to these demands.

It now fell to the SIM to notify senior staff that FIST failed scrutiny, because *Integration* had been ignored. At a time when Nimrod MRA4 and Chinook Mk3 were gaining attention as first class cock-ups, and war had kicked off in Afghanistan, the last thing politicians needed was bad news on the main Infantry 'project'. He was asked what could be done to avoid returning the approval for a complete rethink. His solution was a concept not addressed in any regulation or guideline. He wrote a 'Clarification Paper', proposing it should simply be inserted as an Annex in the User Requirement Document. The process was stabilised. Shortly, a new 13-man 'integration team' was formed to replace him, headed by a Para Colonel. Having no role in this new structure, the SIM left. FIST slowed to a crawl at a crucial time.

By 2006 the notional £4Bn for equipment had been reduced to £600M. The main driver was the need to plug the black hole in the Future Rapid Effects System (FRES) funding, intended to have been a family of armoured or protected vehicles. It, too, underwent many resets, and one of its bastard great-grandchildren, AJAX, is today one of MoD's most embarrassing and enduring failures. What survives of FIST is the Integrated Solider System initiative, with the same aims as those developed by the SIM in 2001. To be still valid over two decades later, through innumerable policy and organisational upheavals, must mean it has proven worth. Better resourced *management* initiatives have been dumped after months or even weeks. For example, Chief of Defence Procurement Instructions.

As for the equipment, the incremental acquisition policy continues, and is seen to operate efficiently, within approved resources. This is in no small way down to the Integrated Soldier System process giving the users direct input at every stage, the basic premise underpinning the first draft plan. While the benefit is difficult to quantify, the casualty rate in Afghanistan was low, and the survival rate high. This is all positive, but one must bear in mind that these soldiers, who in previous decades and centuries would have died, now need care and support. That aspect is most definitely ignored by MoD and government.

Power, greed and corruption - the QinetiQ scandal

MoD(PE) had been forewarned under the Thatcher administration of the intent to overhaul MoD's Research and Development (R&D), employing around 14,000 scientists across 80 sites. In 1991 the Defence Research Agency (DRA) was formed, with famous names such as the Royal Signals and Radar Establishment at Malvern disappearing. In 1995 it subsumed other areas, and became the Defence Evaluation and Research Agency (DERA).

In 1997, and partly in response to complaints from industry that MoD was awarding too much work in-house, the new (New) Labour government sought proposals from the DERA Chief Executive; who suggested R&D should be financed by private capital, while remaining focused on its core roles. Government agreed to operate parts of MoD as a business. Make lots of money for shareholders, paid for by the Defence equipment budget. Twelve years later the entire concept was the subject of severe criticism in the Nimrod Review, which the government claimed to have accepted in full. Yet it persists.

In preparation, a system of 'soft charging' was imposed. Project offices and DERA would for a period go through the motions of negotiating contracts, but no money would change hands. Typical tasks included specialist advice on sophisticated radar designs, where MoD's truly expert scientists at Malvern would assist the project managers. As they always did. But the extra layers of red tape would inevitably lead to delays and cost escalation. As if to ensure this, in 1997 the Chief of Defence Procurement (CDP) issued simultaneously two directives:

1. Henceforth, he was to personally sign all requirements before they were committed to contract; in effect suspending the delegated authority of all his staff.
2. He didn't want engineers managing engineering projects, and announced ~600 were to go.

Plainly, he didn't realise (1) meant he would be conducting Requirement Scrutiny, because he later ruled that doing so was an offence. It soon became apparent through complaints from Main Building that they had not been told their requirements would effectively be frozen while CDP worked his way through scores of submissions every week. Which of course he couldn't, 'pushing right' a huge chunk of defence expenditure.

It was a savings measure by stealth, but the government could say it had not issued an edict to freeze or even slow down expenditure. A veritable windfall, ignoring the bow-wave that was being created. *That's for the next guy. Gimme my gong.*

The *reduction in posts* policy ignored that *someone* had to do the work. Over the next few years an industry of consultants was created, with no mechanism to ensure they actually knew what they were talking about. That's how MoD and government 'savings' work. No mention that it now cost far more, paid from a different budget (the equipment budget, not MoD(PE)'s operating costs, the key deceit). The enforced delays meant previously agreed contracts were no longer valid. Project plans went out the window.

'Soft charging' duly transitioned to 'hard charging', and project offices had to pay in hard cash. The need to negotiate dummy, and then real annual contracts meant a further increase in workload, diverting staff from primary tasks. Inevitably, and to the joy of politicians (because money wasn't being spent), delays mounted. Two-faced, they cried *'delays'* at committee, their outpourings adding up to nothing. Procurers were told they had to find the money within the existing budget, which meant 'salami slicing' the requirement. Whole capabilities would be cut, often making them unviable. Or, numbers cut, increasing the unit cost. (A good example is the current acquisition of 'Wedgetail' to replace the Boeing E-3 Sentry AWACS aircraft. The cost for the original fleet of five was to be £2.155Bn. Five were reduced to three, which will cost £1.89Bn).

In early 2001, Minister for the Armed Forces Dr Lewis Moonie (who later also ruled that refusing to commit fraud was an offence[36]) announced the creation of a commercial company to be owned by MoD, to be called QinetiQ. In June that year DERA became independent of MoD, with around two-thirds of staff incorporated into QinetiQ.

The remainder formed the fully government-owned Defence Evaluation and Technology Laboratory (Dstl). Their role would be to provide independent technical and scientific advice. The project office had to <u>understand</u> that advice, and apply it. The problem was, MoD(PE)'s senior management had declared it didn't want people who

---

36 Letter D/USofS/LM 2214 & 1401/03/Y, 30 April 2003, from Dr Lewis Moonie MP to Steve Webb MP.

understood. Dstl became frustrated at apparently being ignored; but this wasn't because they were thought to be wrong, it was because increasing numbers didn't know they were right.

Savings at all costs was the name of the game; even on safety, which was the primary role of the Aircraft and Armament Evaluation Establishment at Boscombe Down. The immediate delays were calamitous, with front line wondering why their kit was suddenly and indefinitely delayed, when a few months before it had been on schedule. None the wiser, they blamed procurers. Again this thrilled government, who had successfully played one against the other. The media swallowed 'confidential' briefings, and the lies were set in stone.

Timeframe is important. What major projects were relying extensively on, especially, Boscombe Down? Nimrod MRA4 and Chinook HC Mk3. Also, for example, a major safety enhancement was being carried out to Tornado, but the project office could not afford to contract Boscombe to provide independent safety assurance. They tried to go it alone, but eventually hit a wall. Boscombe were belatedly contracted, but a Risk to Life notified by the RAF Director of Flight Safety in 1995 was not corrected until 2010.[37] That is a longer delay than either Nimrod or Chinook, and in a safety sense infinitely more serious, but has never been mentioned by any committee. Odd, isn't it?

Initially, then, there was little money to pay DERA, but things got dramatically worse upon the formation of QinetiQ. Immediately, man-hour rates went up to meet profit targets. But the shadiest aspect was the structure and processes introduced. If a project manager were seeking independent safety assurance on a piece of equipment (an obligation), a report would be issued signed by the DERA project manager on behalf of his Superintendent; the process flexible and efficient. But QinetiQ introduced an impenetrable corporate structure. They now typically required a dozen or more signatures, all with increasing man-hour rates. A 250 hour job at £80 an hour would become 500 at up to £160. (Simplistic. Airworthiness clearance for even a relatively minor modification can cost millions). What added benefit did this bring? None. The most apparent change was reports became inconclusive, invariably having recommendations for further work tacked on the end. *We need another contract. Here's our open-ended quote.* Privately, the staff at the coalface - the scientists and engineers - would admit their original

---

37 Tornado report QinetiQ/AT&E/CR00782/1, December 2002.

report was concise and conclusive. But QinetiQ was there to make money. That the source was the Defence equipment budget, at the expense of critical capability, mattered not.

I'm certainly no expert in corporate governance. But I know what my colleagues and I thought. We were disgusted at this new ethos (both in QinetiQ and MoD), whereby a perfectly good system designed to provide safety assurance to the front line was replaced by corporate greed, and executives (and politicians) who quite simply didn't give a hoot about the end user. MoD was a cash machine. A hole in the wall, on the other side the Services, being robbed blind.

Dr Moonie had stated QinetiQ would remain a British business based in the UK, and that MoD would retain a 'special share' in the company, with safeguards in place to prevent conflicts of interest. While QinetiQ had taken steps to operate on a commercial basis, and saw third parties as its key growth area, by April 2002 around 80% of its business was still derived from MoD. A stock market flotation was mooted for that year, but postponed due lack of investor confidence.

The Chief Executive of DERA and his senior executives, all civil servants, were given a free hand. In late 2002 the Carlyle Group, a US private equity firm, publicly declared its intention to purchase a large stake; in February 2003 acquiring a 33.8% share for £42M. When the floatation took place in 2005, ownership had varied slightly, but was divided between MoD (~56%), Carlyle Group (~31%) and staff (~13%).

In 2007 the National Audit Office conducted an inquiry, to determine whether UK taxpayers received good value for money. It was scathing, the role of QinetiQ's management in negotiating terms with Carlyle slammed. It claimed that taxpayers could have gained *'tens of millions'* more than the £42M; an outlay that grew in value to £372M in less than four years - even more lucrative than the Private Finance Initiative. In particular, it was critical of the incentive scheme given (by themselves) to QinetiQ executives, the 10 most senior gaining £107.5m on an investment of £540,000 in the company's shares. This return of 19,714% was described as *'excessive'*; the understatement of the century.

But few in MoD were content. In 2006 the Future Business Group concluded that QinetiQ were not offering the best source of independent advice. As a test case, they ran a competition to compete a contract on engines, and QinetiQ lost to a small company who performed admirably. This confirmed real savings could be made. But in practice little changed.

A subtlety of the agreement between QinetiQ and MoD/Government was that 'Schedule 18' limited them to manufacturing research models or prototypes, not commercial quantities of military kit. They asked for the restriction to be lifted. The key player in this was the Defence Procurement Agency's Commercial Director, who could grant waivers. Hitherto he had seldom approved them, but his attitude relaxed; to the extent that the Commercial Codes of Practice he had to abide by were (once again) widely ignored, to QinetiQ's benefit. For example, Schedule 18 meant they had to act as a sub-contractor, or at most a partner, in manufacturing contracts. Now, they were afforded the same status as a prime bidder, offered one-to-one briefings on Tenders, and given confidential material that would assist their (and their partners') bids. (See also Group 1 'Power mad').

A further headache arose when QinetiQ demanded of MoD they be handed back Intellectual Property Rights (IPR) to technology and designs they'd developed when part of MoD. This had been a fundamental part of the negotiations when QinetiQ were formed, and MoD's retention was government policy. Staff were thoroughly confused, because only a few years before MoD had been committing money to *acquiring* rights.

High level politics were at play. Minister for Defence Procurement, Lord Drayson, had issued a new Defence Industrial Strategy. The new Chief of Defence Procurement, Sir Peter Spencer, was not as pro-USA as his predecessor, and wanted to face more towards Europe. This was linked to the US policy of protectionism that restricts international trade to protect domestic industries. In other words, an arrangement between the US and UK is not an equal partnership, and any MoD procurer who deals with the US is very aware of the costly damage and delays this causes. Regardless of what we think of ourselves, we are a minor customer and sit at the bottom of a very long waiting list when it comes to deliveries and support.

Spencer and Drayson suggested to the French equivalent of the Defence Procurement Agency that two joint Technology Demonstrator Programmes be established to see how they work out. This was related to the issue of indigenous UK capability, but recognising that a major supplier (Thales) was French, yet employed thousands of UK workers.

An agreement was signed. For current purposes, the point here is that procurement strategies, ostensibly developed by procurers, are very often dictated by political expediencies. The procurers see the pitfalls, but all they can do is enter them in the Risk Register and try to cope.

Shadowplay

One of the unknown pleasures awaiting procurers was that Dstl's remit had been revised to include 'shadowing' QinetiQ. The hypothetical 250 hour task, which had become 500, now had to have a Dstl team 'shadowing' it. Not overseeing or managing it. No executive authority. Just *there*, hovering in the background. It was not entirely clear what their output should actually be. More often than not it was a report saying *We agree with QinetiQ*. (Often they sat in the same office, and more than once it was asked if there was double accounting going on. The kind of question that never gets an answer). They had no need to demand a contract to do further work, as that would automatically follow.

The situation descended into farce. One prime example was on electrical power for dismounted soldiers - a domain I've already discussed. When the FIST project team had been established a deliberate decision was made to recruit a power specialist - a superb and highly qualified engineer. QinetiQ and Dstl were simply not needed (and to be fair, most there agreed).

But the System Integration Manager (SIM) was collared by the Integrated Project Team Leader. Why hadn't he spent that year's £2M budget for 'extramural assistance'? (A lot of man-hours). The answer was it wasn't needed, as the work was being done by the SIM and the young engineer. But it transpired Dstl must also be contracted to 'shadow' work done in-house by these engineers. Everything now had to be pored over by people with no responsibility or accountability, but whose recommendations the project manager must now heed; and explain why if he did not accept them.

Once again - *Who was actually in charge?* Dstl, the aforementioned Integration Authority, or the FIST team leader? The latter, who when appointed believed he would have authority commensurate with his responsibilities, now found himself having to satisfy many masters, each with different agendas, and none helpful.

Jock was on the phone one day to his 'shadow' at Dstl Haslar, Gosport. The subject was portable power, in particular the dangers of Lithium-Ion batteries when struck by a projectile. He knew the effect to be like a violent Roman Candle erupting from the battery casing. (One reason for the 'flaming events').

The floorplate of about 40 civil servants and Army officers was generally quiet, people head down in their work. From Jock's corner, in an impenetrable Glaswegian accent, came *'You're ******* sacked'*, followed by the phone slamming down. The Dstl chap wasn't incompetent, not by a long stretch. But he was trying to undermine Jock's work and position, wanting to start again and run the show, because he was two grades higher.

The floorplate fell silent. Jock looked up at his boss apologetically. Before either could speak, the FIST team leader strolled across. What was going on, and who had Jock 'sacked'? (That is, terminated his contract on that project). The SIM replied, *'Give me a minute and I'll tell you how much time and money he's just saved us'*. Jock was quietly told not to swear so loudly in the future when sacking prats like that, but widely praised by all the infantry officers when word got round what he was trying to achieve. All except the one with his personal integration consultant. Jock responded in his own unique way.

His main job was to manage trials of the Integrated Soldier System output. An enormous task never attempted before on such a scale, and the meetings he chaired were attended by senior Army officers, all intrigued at a young civvy engineer doing this so effortlessly. A critical problem was the soldier's susceptibility to heat stresses - something that unfortunately crops up regularly. The aim is to test human (and equipment) limits, and one receives a medical check after heavy exertion. Jock drafted an update to these procedures, changing oral thermometers to rectal; which of course MoD, being MoD, doesn't actually call rectal, or even anal. It's got a NATO Stock Number, a Part Number, and is called something like 'Instrument, Capillary Tube, Thermal, Innuendo'. His plan was duly signed off, and only afterwards did he send out an e-mail asking what length and thickness the Army preferred, or would they like a range of sizes according to personal tastes. Jock, I wonder how many soldiers your expertise and dedication saved from death or severe injury?

Group 4 - Technical / Industrial

23. *Is it technically feasible judged against the state of the art?*

24. *Has industry the capacity to take on the work?*

25. *Is the maintenance or development of a needed industrial capability consistent with the efficient execution of the project?*

26. *What is the sale potential?*

27. *Has the requirement been overstated (possibly so as to fix on a particular solution)? Is there any acceptable change which would allow competition?*

#23 is for the Provisioning Authority to answer, part of his role being to keep abreast of what's what, and one can let a Feasibility Study to assist. Through this he will be aware of #24. #25 is closely related, as he must profile his bids according to the company's capacity. #27 requires him to have a broad and deep appreciation of the Services' operational intent and usage, what is possible, and what other users have. The project manager must also be able to answer these.

#26 relates in part to Intellectual Property Rights (IPR). The Provisioning Authority must be aware because who owns IPR determines to an extent how many of a given item must be procured. (The IPR owner must provide the Reference Model - see Group 6, later). Also, if MoD owns IPR in full or in part, it will receive a Commercial Exploitation Rate on sales to other users. The project manager agrees this, the question being how much of the design is owned by MoD. The income is usually allocated to non-core requirements.

Rotten to the core

Environmental Test Chambers (ETCs) are used for (wait for it) environmental testing; usually provided by MoD and their use passed between projects. Separately there will be a maintenance contract, and MoD's rules require it to sit with the original manufacturer. At Ferranti, in Edinburgh, MoD had provided around a dozen ETCs, housed in a large purpose-built hangar.

When it came to Eurofighter and Merlin wanting to use them, they were found to be in disrepair; primarily the wooden plinths forming the bases were rotted. They leaked like a sieve. Air Member Supply and Organisation (AMSO) had cancelled the maintenance contracts, their view being they didn't produce anything tangible so were a waste of money. An unrelated project office quietly arranged for them to be repaired and calibrated. Once again, a case of seeking out someone who knew what to do. However, that did not solve the root problem.

Shortly, precisely the same issue arose at Thorn-EMI Varian in Hayes, Middlesex, who made the aforementioned magnetrons for Lynx and Sea Harrier radars. Production was managed carefully around the need to keep the ETCs 'exercised'. If fewer magnetrons were being built, then maintenance activity increased; if only by regularly putting a magnetron through its test procedure. It was a fine balancing act, and worked well.

Thwarted on Eurofighter and Merlin, this time the suppliers took a harder line. Not only did they cancel the maintenance contract, they stopped paying for storage of the ETCs and other test equipment. The company promptly wrote back asking: *'Which car park do you want them dumped in'*. Once again, huge waste was averted only when a project manager told the company to bury costs in a production contract.

But this could only be a temporary salve, and AMSO refused to contemplate a permanent solution. Start-up costs on each new production run increased, and production yield dropped. The production lead time doubled, as did the unit price. Of greater concern, although not to AMSO, shortages worsened at front line.

False economy

The Provisioning Authority had received a routine heads-up from the Chief Petty Officer in charge of the Sea Spray radar bench at RNAS Portland that he was being posted. Portland was the Typed Air Station for Lynx, home to training squadrons and the Lynx that were normally deployed on frigates and destroyers. The Chief's concern was that he had not been tasked with training a replacement. He knew that the Recovery Rate would fall to zero, meaning everything removed from aircraft would be sent back to 3rd Line at Fleetlands. Beyond that he couldn't predict what might happen - that was the Provisioning Authority's job. *He* knew that Fleetlands didn't have the capacity.

This would mean arranging with the project office to increase capacity on the Ferranti contract in Edinburgh. Hard cash would have to be found, because Portland and Fleetlands were funded through different budgets, neither accessible to a project manager. Between them, the Provisioning Authority and project manager estimated an extra £1M per year was required, which proved accurate. The Maintenance Policy had to be restructured. The money was found, but at the expense of other requirements.

It matters not how long ago this was. The main lessons are the disproportionate cost of changing the Maintenance Policy, and that chopping one post cost a *recurring* £1M a year. The RN trumpeted this as a saving. The real cost was, and remains, loss of flexibility.

Dig deeper

While we're on Sea Spray, Fleetlands had demanded 10 of a minor component in the Transmitter (a transformer), a figure arrived at after surveying and testing units received from Portland. But AMSO hadn't maintained their stock levels and didn't have any. (The 'Not in Time' policy). Their 'system' (such as it was) required the supply manager to provide the next highest assembly, in this case the Transmitter itself. But of course there were none serviceable - and in any case what's the point of sending Fleetlands a Transmitter to repair... a Transmitter? AMSO decided 10 should be bought, at over £85k each. But their computer was programmed to flag there were five main units comprising the radar. They raised a requisition, endorsed to the tune of £3.626M. Within weeks a similarly erroneous requisition for £3.840M was raised to procure Sea King radar equipment. The project manager ripped them up. Instead, he bought a batch of transformers for about £5k. (Nothing was needed on Sea King). AMSO dug their heels in, would not release the funding for other requirements, and it was lost. (Under MoD's then financial rules it could not be carried forward).

This was recurring, on all avionics. The project manager just happened to be familiar with Sea Spray from a previous post. But when canvassed, his colleagues all conceded they would have let both contracts. That was not their fault, because lacking direct knowledge they had to trust that the Service HQ had conducted scrutiny and endorsed the buy. After all, it was *their* money.

It would be boring and repetitive to map each failure to the *Steps*, but it can be seen these fail *Step #1 - 'Why is it needed?'* Answer - *It's not.* Seven and a half million saved by a couple of phone calls and 10 minutes to scribble out a requisition for the transformers. Nobody asked *How?* or *Why?* It was just too embarrassing to admit, never mind publicise so lessons could be learned. Flag Officer Naval Air Command staff were delighted at having their Lynx fleet fully fitted. Yet from top to bottom of AMSO the project manager was gaslighted. Told he was utterly and completely wrong, despite Fleetlands pushing out 10 serviceable Transmitters within days of receiving the transformers. Was this a rarity? Not by any means. In fact, it was a was a daily occurrence.

Two way street

In October 1971 NATO announced that the Microwave Aircraft Digital Guidance Equipment (MADGE) developed by MEL (Mullard Equipment Limited) and Mullard Research Laboratories had won the competition to select a new tactical approach and landing aid. In doing so it beat off proposals from Germany, France and the US Air Force. It was trialled successfully in Westland Wessex, Vickers Varsity and Avro 748. The government announced it planned to equip around 1,000 Navy, Army and RAF aircraft and provide 90 ground stations. Contracts were let to mature the basic concept.

Fast forward and the first customer was RN Sea Harriers, with carriers having a complementary onboard system, and a transportable ground system to be taken ashore when conducting littoral operations. Various upgrades were developed... A Data Acquisition and Transmission System (DATS) passed the ship's course and speed to the aircraft's NAVHARS (Navigation and Heading Reference System). Without this, the pilot's workload increased enormously. A Microwave Dummy Deck Landing System (MDDLS) was installed at RNAS Yeovilton to practice deck landings. And a Near Field Integrity Monitoring System (NFIMS) was used to monitor the integrity of the transportable system at low elevation angles (<1.5°). The fundamental complexity of MADGE will be apparent. Both aircraft and 'airfield' were moving. This was seriously expensive kit, and crucial to planned carrier operations.

Let's get MDDLS out of the way first, because that's what the RN did. A naval rating at Yeovilton reversed a 4-ton truck over it.

The Maintenance Policy... A full 2nd Line repair facility would be established at Yeovilton, the Sea Harrier Typed Air Station, but a limited capability on the carriers. There would be no 3rd Line (MoD civilian workshops), but a 4th Line contact would be let on MEL. This was consistent with RN Fixed Wing support policy.

Automatic Test Equipment suites were required. (Six foot high 19" racks). MEL had developed their own in parallel with the main equipment. Using this, MADGE had been qualified and Certificates of Design issued. Like most such equipment at this stage, it was of 'breadboard' standard, and unsuitable for Service use. A contract would be required to make it compatible with the enhancements, productionise it, and buy more. To have anyone but MEL do this would be more or less insane.

MoD contracted Graseby Dynamics (well known for their excellent chemical agent monitors used by troops).

Plainly, MEL would have to be paid to ensure the Graseby design evolved with the ongoing enhancements. Instead, Graseby were left to their own devices; delivering two suites reflecting the MADGE build standard at time of contract award, not at time of delivery. The work was never completed, the contracts paid-off.

In the Navigation project office the imperative was self-preservation. The 'solution' was to divert attention by transferring *all* navigation production and repair contracts, over 600 of them, to the Fire Control and Surveillance Radar office. What did this achieve? Under MoD rules the previous staff could no longer be required to answer for their mistakes. They were under no obligation to even offer a hand-over, and didn't. Yes, it really is that straight-forward. If you screw up and want to avoid awkward questions, just get your boss to transfer the contract to another office. Or swap jobs with the guy sitting next to you.

(Indeed, this concept has been tested in court on a number of occasions, each time the Coroner allowing MoD to refuse to answer questions on the grounds that the witness, <u>chosen by MoD</u>, was not in post at the time. Most recently, in November 2021 in the death of Corporal Jon Bayliss. Similarly, the Information Commissioner has ruled it a valid reason for refusing to answer Freedom of Information requests. Hence, any committee, court or Inquiry has great difficulty extracting the information it needs, rendering its work of limited value).

The new project manager quickly discovered this was the least of his problems. The US Department of Defense had been on the verge of buying MADGE for the aircraft used to fly the US President. This would have been the biggest order MEL had ever received. The more expensive ground/ship-based part of the system was to be located in every State, and on every ship capable of taking the aircraft. (Whereas the RN had a mere handful). The previous project manager had accompanied MEL to a presentation at the Pentagon. The senior officer present had asked of him: *'What does the MoD think of MADGE?'*. *'Don't buy it, it's unreliable'*. End of presentation.

On 11 September 1990 the Board of Directors were allowed to 'interview' the new project manager. A unique occurrence.

'Does the new MADGE project manager agree with his predecessor that our equipment is unreliable?'

'No, it's not unreliable, it's unavailable'.

Upon explaining why, he was invited to contribute to a briefing for the UK Ambassador so that the US Department of Defense could be lobbied to reconsider. It wouldn't budge. Displaying remarkable restraint, MEL did not seek redress.

Unreliable or unavailable? It had taken less than a day in post to suss the reason. The supply branch looking after RN equipment, SM47 (yes, them again), had decided to save on repair costs by simply scrapping much of MADGE. It achieved this by changing stores classifications from Permanent (repairable) to Consumable, and transferring management to SS51; who looked after high volume/low cost consumables, not low volume/high cost Line Replaceable Units costing upwards of £100k each. Gradually, equipment developed faults and was returned for repair. (Salt water is a harsh environment for electronics, and the carriers' antenna system was unavoidably open to the elements on the Quarterdeck). Whoever signed this off committed fraud.

To a young Administrative Assistant in SS51, any kit is just a NATO Stock Number on a computer. Their 'system' simply churns out an automatic requisition when a predetermined stock level is reached, and they send it to the relevant procurement office who are expected to have the funding. But of course they didn't. Again, *Step #1 - Why is it needed? It isn't*. The *actual* requirement was to spend a fraction of the money on repairs. In other words, meet the Maintenance *Policy*, upon which all materiel and financial provision is based.

So confusing was the situation to SS51 staff, on 9 February 1991 they ordered spares to the value of £1,924,731, to replace those scrapped under DM87. Again, a *Step #1* failure, because under AMSO's new rules there could be no legitimate use, and once delivered would also be scrapped. Swiftly, the RN was down to a partial squadron fitted; becoming academic when no carrier was equipped.

The £5 plug

While all this was going on, the project manager received a call from a Sea Harrier Board of Inquiry President asking why MADGE hadn't been fitted to the aircraft; meaning the pilot couldn't get home to the carrier safely after a bird strike damaged other sensors. He related the above - the RAF was in the process of scrapping the kit.

The Captain shuddered. At his behest the project manager convened a meeting in London, where he demanded of suppliers why they had ordered millions of pounds worth of equipment to be scrapped for the sake of simple repairs. Emphasising his point, he demonstrated a 5-minute repair to a £100k Transponder, replacing a £5 Reynolds connector on the Travelling Wave Tube (TWT). The suppliers' response was to scrap the stock of connectors. *We can do what we want, the Navy has no say.* Flag Officer Naval Air Command staff were stunned, but now knew why only a half a squadron was fitted. Captain Chris Esplin-Jones RN wrote: *'This is an indictment on the way we conduct business'.*[38]

The following day the project manager drove his car to Yeovilton, picked up 25 TWTs, and took them nearly 200 miles to the English Electric Valves factory in Witham. Of these 25, costing over of £10k each and which the RAF had ordered to be scrapped, 19 were recovered for a total of £5k; either by replacing the said connectors or by spot-knocking (a method of hardening the tubes if they have been unused for a period - in simple terms, burning off internal residue). The cost was charged to another MoD contract at the company. The RN was back up to two squadrons. Only one to go. But AMSO persisted, scrapping perfectly good kit and concealing the scale of their waste. That's one way of managing a budget. Another is to stop pouring money down the drain

---

38 The Esplin Islands in Antarctica were named after Captain Esplin-Jones, then a Sub-Lieutenant, after his Hydrographic Survey Group charted them in 1962/3. Twenty years later, as a Commander, he piloted the MV Norland into San Carlos Water under enemy fire to disembark 2 Para for their advance on Goose Green. A few days later he repeated the feat with the Gurkhas.

and make the aircraft safe.

The end is nigh

On 10 September 1991, a change in postholder saw the RN's Sea Harrier office announce *'If reliability is high enough, we won't need 2nd Line'*. This completely ignored the more pressing issue of AMSO scrapping the kit. All MADGE arisings at 1st Line would be now returned to 4th Line. That is, similar to the aforementioned demise of the Sea Spray radar facility at Portland. But there was more MADGE equipment, and it was more complex and costly to repair. And to have no repair capability on carriers would require an increase in spare systems they would have to carry - which would need to be procured. There had been no scrutiny.

In this certain knowledge, a quite deliberate decision was taken to waste money. It was spun as a 'saving', no longer having the expense of running the Yeovilton and carrier benches. Like the suppliers, the RN took no account of the much greater cost that would now have to be borne by a different part of the RN budget, which was based on an assumed 80% Recovery Rate at 2nd Line. Now it was to be 0%. This 2nd Line Recovery Rate is the single most important factor in aircraft support. The rule of thumb is anything under 50% requires aircraft robbery. Any reduction automatically requires an uplift in funding. None was provided.

Such a policy change requires Investment Appraisal, approval granted to cancel and pay-off contracts, and confirmation that the uplift has been approved. And then a period of transition. The RN did none of this. It issued no formal notification, MEL finding out when a truckload of MADGE turned up for repair - which the suppliers had already decided was now consumable, and for which there was no longer any contractual cover. The saving grace was this truckload was now under the control of the project manager, who refused to scrap it.

If anyone in MoD doesn't understand that 80% to zero will cause problems, then there is no hope.

A minor diversion in Lagos

There are some companies that go the extra mile. MEL were one. A component in RAF surveillance radars, a thyristor, had become obsolete. A contract had been let on Thomson-CSF in France (essentially the production arm of the French Ministry of Defence, but who had bought MEL Communications). Mere days before the delivery date, and having given routine updates assuring MoD and MEL everything was fine and the new design worked, they pulled the plug entirely; leaving the UK high and dry. Down to a few weeks stock, the RAF's long range Search and Rescue (SAR) capability would soon be extremely limited. Questions would be asked in the House.

MEL's Marketing Director, Ian Loakes, made it his mission to solve the problem. A few weeks later he called the project manager from a backstreet shop in Lagos, where he had tracked down an old shipment from Westinghouse, the original manufacturer. Over a bad line he told him the price - £250. There was a crate of over 200, about 15 years supply. The project manager said *'Buy'*. Fifty grand was a no-brainer to keep SAR going. When the invoice arrived, it was for Ian's flight and expenses, and £250 for the whole crate.

A guy walks into a pub...

OMEGA was a hyperbolic navigation system, replaced by GPS. The main standing task was the 18-monthly software update to reflect changes in the Earth's geo-magnetic field. The work was carried out by Ferranti Radar Systems in Edinburgh, their engineers using old BBC micro-computers paid for by MoD.

Anyone who ever used a BBC will know that for every hour they worked, many more hours of blood, sweat, tears, swearing and a 5lb club hammer were required to keep them going. A unique and strictly off-the-books support arrangement existed. In exchange for their evening computer club being allowed to use the BBCs, Ferranti would support them free of charge; the additional benefit to MoD being there would always trained programmers available. But the BBC was fast becoming obsolete and unsupportable. (The computer that is, but could equally apply...). The project manager (who was also the Technical Agency) agreed to fund three IBM PCs to replace the BBCs, justifying this as a spend-to-save measure; something entirely within his gift. That year's upgrade was delivered on time, and worked perfectly; embodied by the RAF at 30MU Sealand. The BBCs were donated to a school.

Meanwhile, the project manager's boss had reached the ripe old age of 60 and so had to retire; or, if he wished, drop a grade and stay on. He chose the latter, and his replacement was a former Army officer whose first job it was in procurement. Shortly, he called the project manager into his office. *'I believe you manage something called OMEGA?'*. Receiving confirmation, he directed that all contracts with Ferranti be cancelled forthwith, and transferred to a company near Heathrow. Asked for justification, he replied that he'd met his new neighbour *'For a drink and a chat in the pub last night, and he reckons he can do the job. So, crack on and I'll let him know to expect the contracts later this week'*.

The project manager refused, but could not avoid the possibility that at contract renewal there might be a legitimate alternative, so would have to vet them. He took himself off to Heathrow, discovering that the 'company' was a one-man and his dog operation - literally - in a single rented room in a small office block. Asked who would actually do the work should his bid succeed, the friendly neighbour happily announced he'd sub-contract it to his mate who ran a small automotive engineering firm on the same trading estate. Ferranti continued to do an excellent job until OMEGA left service.

Please Sir

There were three Nimrod R1 ELINT (Electronic Intelligence) aircraft, with one always in a hangar at RAF Wyton undergoing upgrade and scheduled maintenance. This, because the average lifespan of a given ELINT system was around 18 months, it being necessary to continually monitor and counter the opposition's own capabilities. A never ending job. After a long capability gap caused by Nimrod being withdrawn from service in 2011, the R1s were replaced with RC-135W Rivet Joints (or Airseeker), the last of the three delivered in 2017. It is not a like-for-like replacement, inferior in some respects, superior in others.

When Saddam Hussein invaded Kuwait on 2 August 1990, the ELINT equipment project manager was called to a briefing in Main Building. For the first time all three R1s were to be operational together; drop dead date, first week in November. To get the aircraft ready would 'simply' involve doing the job more quickly at Wyton, meaning 24/7 shift work. But the difficulty on ELINT equipment was that, because of the short lifespan, only enough kit for the two flying aircraft was ever bought. Now, a full suite of the 39 systems would have to be produced and fitted inside 12 weeks.

The one thing not mentioned was money. Nimrod R was the nearest thing MoD had to a 'money no object' job, but it still had to be found. The project manager contacted RAF Strike Command's Financial &

Secretariat (F&S) Branch at High Wycombe, headed by a middle ranking civil servant. Asked to identify in-year funds he refused, saying *'I require a personal letter from Mrs Thatcher saying we're going to war'*. He was later rewarded with an invite to a No.10 garden party, although Mrs Thatcher had been replaced by John Major so he couldn't regale her with his efficiency. Never mind, rumour had it he was personally decorated by Saddam for his contribution to the Iraqi war effort.

Instead, that afternoon the project manager let 39 contracts by faxed A5 memo, asking each company to accept his word that payment would follow in due course. Not one demurred, although a firm in Coventry were found to have entered receivership. A squad of civvies was despatched in a mini-bus, blagged their way past security and receivers, and removed all MoD equipment.

The problematic equipment was Direction Finding Spinners, the various sized antennae fitted in the aircraft's bomb bay. Box-like structures, they were heavy and very awkward to remove from the aircraft during servicing. Accidental damage was common, so this was one equipment where MoD had spares; but they were all at Ferranti awaiting repair. There had been no great priority placed on them, but Saddam's south-east excursion changed all that.

The only spare of the largest antenna had been dropped, and was badly damaged and holed. Only the project manager and MoD's Resident Quality Assurance Officer were authorised to agree concessions to repair schemes. The former convened a Local Equipment Repair Committee to agree an acceptable repair standard and get the work under way immediately. One difficulty was getting hold of the chief hydraulic engineer, who was on holiday and found up a church tower in Dundee effecting repairs to the clock as part of his hobby. The necessary repair was essentially a huge blob of epoxy-like material bonded over the damage. One then had to dynamically balance the antenna - a direct analogy being when Kwik-Fit add lead weights to balance a wheel. Only this time the blob weighed kilos. If not balanced correctly, when first spun-up in the bomb bay at around 300 rpm the aircraft would shake alarmingly on its jacks.

Simple enough, but... The main reason repairs were scheduled for Xmas and summer was the only computer system that could do the job was owned by West Lothian Education Authority, and could only be loaned to MoD/Ferranti during school holidays. In Scotland August is too late, as they break up a month earlier than the rest of the UK, traditionally

111

and ostensibly to allow the kids to go berry picking. Saddam's timing was impeccable. Negotiations opened with the Education Authority. Its leader quickly and without question agreed to an immediate loan, a decision he knew would cause turmoil in school.

The project manager decided MoD should own a capability. Bearing in mind F&S's attitude, he told Ferranti to buy a system (hardware, software, building works, training, support) and charge it as 'materiel' to an RN contract that had an underspend. The kids were back in business.

The third Rl flew on time. The Education Authority leader did not get invited to No.10, but he did receive a letter of grateful thanks. At the time MoD denied the existence of the Rl, so the letter had to be couched accordingly. If he's reading this, a penny might drop! Well done Sir.

The lesson? Ignore those in senior positions who have authority but no responsibility. They serve no useful purpose. Get rid.

A question of time

The critical path to flying the third Rl was a Multi-Band Receiving System, part of which was repaired at Cossor, Harlow. (For security reasons the components comprising ELINT systems were supplied by disparate contactors). The entire task was endangered by the lack of a simple Junction Box.

At a meeting held days after the invasion, the repair manager was bullish. *No, it won't be ready for November, and when it is it's going to cost you £xxk*. The project manager adjourned, saying they would reconvene at the repair bench after coffee, so he could have a look. Companies aren't used to this. Upon arrival, he took hold of a screwdriver and removed the top plate. Looking inside, it was clear the burnt-out wiring loom would have to be replaced. The repair manager pointed out its complexity, and the sheer number of soldered and crimped joints in the connectors. *See? We have to manufacture a new loom. £xxk*. The project manager reached for the Illustrated Parts Catalogue. They're not used to that either. He pointed out the complete loom was a referenced item, and spares had been bought for Cossor's sole use. One learns this from the Class of Store column. (C/3 - Consumable, and replaced at 3rd Line or beyond). On Rl ELINT equipment there was no 3rd Line. Upon checking, it was ascertained the stocks had not yet been scrapped under DM87, so the job was man-hours only.

The repair manager was told to get on with it, and report back in one hour. He confirmed the Box would be ready the following evening; *but the quote stood*. If you've done this type of work before, you know *exactly* how long it takes. The project manager turned to the contracts manager and offered him £300 for three hours work. Not a penny more. He agreed, and RAF Wyton picked the Box up two days later.

The RAF were present throughout. *Can you do this for all our kit you manage? Yes. But who's going to do this on other kit?* No-one mate. You'll be wasting money for ever more. Look after the pennies...

Smart(er) Acquisition

'Faster, cheaper, better', proclaimed the Chief of Defence Procurement. But he didn't lay down any benchmarks or targets. Asked for guidelines on our domain, we were advised that if endorsement to delivery of first items could be reduced by, say, 18 months, that would be good. We pointed out that the ELINT equipment had a typical life of 18 months, and to take longer than three months from endorsement to delivery was considered poor.

The committees viewed this in black and white. *Projects failed because they were managed pre-Smart Acquisition. Thereafter, there could be nothing but success. It was the panacea.* Today, they bang on about learning lessons from the Urgent Operational Requirement (UOR) process, which allows certain shortcuts. That would certainly be a good first step - so long as they acknowledge it is but a small step. It remains a constant source of frustration, both to procurers and front line, that successful procurement and support models like ELINT are rejected. Why? What motives drive the decision makers? The only conclusion I can come to, and it has been admitted to me many times by senior staff, is that they cannot contemplate the bar being raised.

The needs of the many

A novel and contentious project had been given to procurers shortly after 9/11: arising from confidential briefings and warnings given to Prime Minister Tony Blair about the threat of 'dirty bombs' - revealed officially only recently (July 2023) when sealed government documents were released. Minor in financial terms, but any delay would upset Ministers and foreign governments. A number of failed attempts had been made, and delivery was already late, when in 2003 it was handed to yet another project manager to give it a go.

The stumbling block was the system had to include a feature whereby a senior officer, watching what the operators were doing via a video link, would be able to press a button setting off an explosive device (hopefully) neutralising the threat, but killing his 4-man team. Most reasonable people appreciate that sacrifice of a few is sometimes necessary. But who was going to sign-off on this? Formal acceptance should have been provided, but it wasn't mentioned.

Two years previously the Army had said in broad terms, that could be interpreted in dozens of ways:

We want something to do this... Here's £4.5M.

Now, asked for more detail, they said:

We've costed each system at £1M, we want 20, and we want them in three months. And the total cost must not exceed the £4.5M.

They didn't say *what* they'd costed, or from whom. Asked, they replied:

You've only got two months now... and the budget is still £4.5M.

After examining what the systems might comprise, what they had to be integrated with (existing emergency services and the Cabinet Office Briefing Rooms), and where they had to be deployed (anywhere in the UK, at the drop of a hat), it was clear they would need a transport fleet; but the Army had overlooked this. Also, clearance to be carried in certain aircraft, which would have to be on constant stand-by - easily the single most expensive item. And an all-new support infrastructure was needed, extending to real estate to store and maintain these classified systems near potential high-risk targets.

The initial assessment quickly got to £60M, plus aviation, infrastructure and through-life costs; meaning the requirement moved up two Categories in financial terms and would need to be resubmitted for re-approval. Told this, the Army replied:

We've cut your £4.5M to £1.5M, and we want all 20 next week.

No, you can't make this up.

Put yourself in the shoes of the project manager. Given the case studies I've offered, the associated policies, and the prevailing culture, what would you have done? This would make an excellent exam question at project manager training courses or interviews. Solve it (not by cancellation!), and you won't struggle with many other problems. *You've got 10 minutes to come up with a plan. Go...*

Group 5 - Modifications

28. Is the modification required to make the equipment work and, if so, what is the cost and the effect on timescales?

29. Is it an enhancement?

The questions are intended for the *initial* scrutiny stage, and address a basic principle of Defence procurement. If one is 'merely' seeking to maintain the build standard of an already delivered equipment, then one develops the modification under Post Design Services. (PDS, defined as *Maintaining the Build Standard*. See Group 6). Very often it is convenient to include embodiment in the task if the cost is minimal, or requires the specialist skills of the Post Design Contractor's engineers.

If the requirement doesn't meet this criteria then it is an enhancement, requiring a separately endorsed and funded requirement, but which may still be carried out under PDS. In fact, one must give good reason *not* to, as the basic process is the same. The only difference is the source of funding. Failure to grasp this distinction, and adopt the correct development strategy, accounts for many delays and cost overruns. In the next Group I will discuss the later approval of individual modifications, where more detailed scrutiny is applied.

The mandated procedures are set out in Defence Standard 05-125/2, including an approved list of reasons for modifying Defence equipment.[39] So, for modifications the answer to *Step #1 - Why is it needed?* must be from that list; which the scrutiny instructions don't mention, rather assuming the scrutineer already knows.

Modifications to Defence equipment account for around a fifth of the annual equipment budget, and that will continue increasing as MoD pursues incremental acquisition strategies. There is nothing wrong with this so long as one makes correct compensatory provision, but too often the gaps between increments result in fragmented capability, or none at all. And invariably loss of corporate knowledge. The greatest danger is when increments are not integrated properly with existing kit, leaving

---

39 Defence Standard 05-125/2, Chapter 7.2.1.

them functionally unsafe. This has killed many.

Until June 1991 the HQ Modifications Committees provided independent scrutiny and oversight; and the *39 Steps* are written on this assumption. But when they were closed down, and the modification sponsor (usually the Service Engineering Authority) was allowed to scrutinise his own requirements and mark his own homework, the system irretrievably broke down - and this remains the case.

Some of the work is obviously still done, but is uncoordinated and fragmented across MoD with practitioners rarely seeing the bigger picture. However, even when the correct process existed, the Services still abused it through inappropriate use of the Service Modification system - which is what it says, a modification designed in-house, and seen as a way of bypassing independent scrutiny, safety assurance, oversight and approval. I'll offer one brief example that resulted in the deaths of two RAF aircrew, and the loss of their aircraft...

Blue on Blue

At 0248 hours local time on 23 March 2003, Flight Lieutenants Kevin Main and David Williams were returning to the Ali Al Salem Air Base, Kuwait, when their Tornado GR4A ZG710 was shot down by a US PATRIOT missile battery. The Battery had arrived in theatre without its equipment and was allocated a partial set of spares. It did not have voice or data links with its Command HQ or other Batteries, and was not part of the integrated air defence network; meaning it was forced to act autonomously. It was not fit for purpose. Flying at around 18,000 feet, in congested airspace, ZG710 was mistaken for an Iraqi Anti-Radiation Missile. The Battery had interrogated the target with its Identification Friend or Foe (IFF) but received no response. The extant US Rules of Engagement allowed it to engage the target in self-defence, but did not provide adequate defence against the possibility of friendly fire.

The Board of Inquiry noted many contributory factors. Primarily: firing doctrine, crew training, IFF procedures, aircraft routing and airspace control measures. Many of these were US liabilities, but the Board did not record what actions the US Inquiry recommended. However, it did criticise the criteria programmed into PATRIOT, which omitted the possibility of an airborne IFF being unserviceable or unavailable.

A design feature within the IFF detects failures and routes a signal to the warning system. The logic is simple. For example: *I have been interrogated. Have I responded correctly? Yes. (Okay). No. (Warn crew, who take action).* As this can be an audio and/or visual cue, the output from the IFF itself is generally a simple switching signal requiring integration with other aircraft systems. But it hadn't been. Plainly, if a specified safety feature has not been integrated properly, the installation does not meet the required performance or safety standards.

The IFF had been embodied by Service Modification, but had not been the subject of a safety assessment - a typical 'savings'. Lacking this, there was no lawful authority to fly. One might reasonably point out we were at war, so *in extremis* rules could be waived. Correct, but IFF is a No Go system. More fundamentally, the problem had been identified four years earlier by another project office, as the same had happened to their aircraft. Formal notifications and then complaints to 2-Star level were rejected. Motive? The same 2-Star was directly responsible for Nimrod MRA4 and Chinook. If he accepted the systemic nature of the violations, and the recommendation to make Tornado safe, it would draw attention to the true reason for the Chinook ZD576 debacle - the aircraft wasn't airworthy. Despite clear risks to life by friendly fire and mid-air collision, his focus was on shutting the scrutineer down.

Withdrawal symptoms

Latterly, the Naval Aircraft Repair Organisation (NARO) comprised two 3rd Line establishments, the Royal Naval Aircraft Workshop Almondbank near Perth, Scotland, and Royal Naval Aircraft Yard Fleetlands in Gosport, England. If a modification programme of any kind was planned, the Provisioning Authority notified his Repair Programmes section, who would task the workshops; paid from the Rotary Wing Support budget. No funding need be sought by the project office.

Commencing the mid-1980s there was much lobbying to do away with 3rd Line altogether. A decade later it was decided NARO would become an Agency of MoD, its work to be paid for with hard cash by project offices; in the same way DERA was restructured. Likewise, in 1999 it was privatised, bought by Vector Aerospace. The loss of flexibility caused far reaching problems that persist to this day.

The Rotary Wing Support budget was not divvied up. It was taken as a 'saving', yet plainly a significant uplift in project funding was required; and, of course, the work now had to be managed by the project office, not the Service HQ. Project managers were told to find the money from existing resources; meaning, yet again, 'salami slicing' something from the requirement. This was one of the largest ever stealth cuts to the Defence equipment budget. (And you will perhaps recall this is exactly what had happened earlier when 2nd Line was run down). In effect, the push was on to change all Maintenance Policies to 1st » 4th Line. Not because it was cheaper or better, but because it off-loaded the problem onto another budget holder - despite him not having any funding.

To fully understand the impact we must return to the actions of Air Member Supply and Organisation (AMSO). When they became Air Member Logistics (AML) in 1994 one of their first acts was to deny NARO access to what remained of MoD's support infrastructure, which they relied upon for Air Publication amendments, obsolescence solving, replies to Query Notes, Fault Investigations, advice and assistance, software updates for Automatic Test Equipment, etc. When NARO became an MoD Agency, the RN's Aircraft Support Executive fell into line with the RAF, making an *executive* decision to stop *supporting* RN *aircraft*. At which point they became pointless.

This was an extension of something I mentioned earlier, the RAF's juvenile refusal to support RN progress meetings if the RN were present. Now, both pulled the plug on RN workshops (which also repaired RAF equipment and aircraft), no longer affording them access to core services; or spares that had been bought for their sole use, which were then scrapped. In effect, a repeat of the DM87 policy. How could NARO meet its commitments? It had been given no notice, and no compensatory funding. The damage knowingly and quite deliberately inflicted was still evident when I retired many years later. It was an abuse of authority. It was sabotage. The only dissenting voices were AML's own avionic project managers, and the Fleetlands Avionic Business Unit Manager. He'd been a Provisioning Authority, so was one of very few at the establishment who could join the dots and see the pitfalls.

One good example occurred on a helicopter upgrade programme. The project was within cost and ahead of schedule, but now had to find the money to pay NARO, who had accepted a 25,000 man-hours task to modify avionic equipment - kit they already repaired. And an even bigger task to modify the 46 aircraft. But, forced into a corner, they advised the project manager they were withdrawing, stating *'We no longer regard MoD(PE) as a customer'*. The project manager was forced to contract industry at huge cost.

Fleetlands' Chief Executive, retired Air Commodore Stephen Hill (no relation), was in an invidious position. His 'Blue Book', whereby the forward loading of his shop floors was scheduled, looked healthy. In fact, these 'initiatives' were effectively cancelling the work left, right and centre. Shortly he would have to consider redundancies. What struck those concerned was Air Commodore Hill had been the Director of Support Management responsible for the RAF's Tornado Force, and was now being royally shafted by his former colleagues. One could look at this another way. His inability to make them see sense indicates the level of support the policy enjoyed. Either way, his old Service left him high and dry, with a major headache.

With no project receiving compensatory funding, many were suddenly over budget. But they were within a fair and reasonable cost for the new requirement. In this case, a job that was heading for an underspend was at the very last moment told to find an extra 20% for services that, when the funding was approved, were not attributable. The trouble was, 95% of the budget had already been spent.

No committee dare mention the decisions that forced this. The self-servers who 'achieved' the savings basked in their new found glory, having totally screwed front line; while the reproved project managers struggled manfully to maintain operational capability. It was very obvious that somewhere on high the question had been asked: *How can we make 3rd Line look inefficient?* Answer: *Stop their ability to meet commitments.*

I'm afraid MoD is not geared to dealing with such events. The 'system' rather assumes the decision has been made on high, by committee. The Services are taught *'Don't fight the white'*, a reference to government policy White Papers. And despite the legal obligation to challenge through Requirement Scrutiny, doing so is fraught with danger. Most turn their backs and hope for the best.

Privatisation is usually 'justified' as a means of introducing market discipline and efficiency to reinvigorate an apparently failing area. The argument is essentially economic, largely ignoring the pain. Was NARO failing? Absolutely not. It was one of MoD's gems, and to a man every civilian engineer was superbly trained. (As they were in the equivalent RAF and Army establishments). The greatest loss was that it was the natural recruitment ground for HQ staff, especially Engineering Authorities and Provisioning Authorities, because their training meant they could easily slot into more senior posts with minimal fuss. That breadth and depth of experience bred intuitive understanding of how to get the job done, but has been replaced with a slow, even lethargic approach, and a degree of risk aversion bordering on terror.

A major flaw in the rush to privatisation is not comparing like with like. For example, today most aircraft maintenance contracts are availability-based and incentivised. If the contractor achieves a given target, say 50% of the fleet, then they are paid top rate. But they are not measured against the expectations placed upon MoD staff when *they* did the job. Then, the requirement was expressed as the maximum number of aircraft in the 'repair pool' of 14%. This was laid down in the Long Term Costings Permanent Instructions, linked to the aforementioned 80% Recovery Rate, and set funding levels. A level playing field requires industry to be placed under the same strictures. Tell them to keep the repair pool under 14% and see what the quote is!

But to his eternal credit, new Defence Committee member Dave Doogan MP, a former MoD apprentice and engineer, said to me:

'Key amongst your observations is the strategic blunder to denude MoD of its own in-house alternative to industry. Not only does MoD consistently exhibit an absence of an Intelligent Client mindset, but has now no other option than to fall at the feet of industry'.[40]

But he's an SNP MP, so will be treated with contempt by the rest of the committee and MoD. *SNP and correct? We can't have that.* And no, I'm not Scottish, but he doesn't hold that against me.

---

40 E-mail Doogan/Hill, 7 December 2022 18:16.

Group 6 - Post Design Services (PDS)

30. Should it have been done under development contracts?

31. How much does it cost in relation to the future life of the equipment?

32. What are the cost/manpower implications of any subsequent modification programme?

33. What is the priority?

#30 could be phrased better, asking for a positive statement that a PDS task has been considered; this being more efficient.

#31 refers in part to the '5-year rule', whereby funding reduces by 20% in each of the five remaining years of life. In general, an Investment Appraisal is required.

#32 is often forgotten - the act of embodiment and ensuring kit can be put to its intended use.

#33 informs the HQ Modification Committee chairman as to the Classification to give a modification.

#32 and #33 are closely linked, and from them emerge the embodiment strategy. The question of *when* it will be embodied in part determines the procurement strategy.

PDS and Modifications (Group 5) are inextricably linked, and the same key players answer the questions and manage the process. But they are given separate groupings for one very good reason. Uniquely across the seven Groups, Requirement Scrutiny of PDS is vested <u>directly with specialists in the field</u>, the Technical Agencies. They, too, are unique, for two reasons:

1. They are formally <u>appointed</u> and named in the contract.
2. They <u>appoint</u> PDS Officers at Design Authorities, who (also uniquely) are given authority to commit MoD funding without seeking approval from the Technical Agency each time. In this way, urgent safety work can commence immediately.

My view is that if one is not prepared to be named in the contract, and accept this responsibility, then that should be a bar to advancement. I acknowledge that would create difficulties elsewhere, as there is no equivalent situation in most fields. Nevertheless, it is indicative of who is really important in Defence acquisition - those who make the decisions and are answerable for them. MoD likes to say it has Senior Responsible Owners for every requirement, but it never mentions the subordinates who are actually named in contracts and called to account.

Reinforcing this, not one of the examples of waste I mention was managed by someone who had been a Technical Agency. All of the successes were. This emphasises a truism; a project manager who has worked his way *backwards* through the Acquisition Cycle, particularly if he has been a Technical Agency, will seldom blunder, and will know the solution to most problems.

To recap, PDS is defined as *Maintaining the Build Standard*. The primary output is a valid Safety Case; which is based on a specific build standard; in turn based on a stated use. If either changes, the Safety Case must be updated. I've explained this hasn't been funded policy for 30 years, and is the principal reason why MoD could not demonstrate, to the respective Reviews, that Nimrod or Chinook were airworthy.

When a design is deemed sufficiently mature, it is brought Under Ministry Control; meaning the Design Authority may no longer change the design unilaterally. The key hurdle is the Transfer to PDS meeting. There is a 4-page checklist; a single failure is sufficient to stop the process in its tracks, and indicates a breakdown in the Defence Lines of Development. (That is, the checklist is a constant reference throughout the project's life. One can use a red/amber/green traffic light system to constantly monitor compliance). If achieving transfer is set as a key aim in any project plan, with a milestone payment, you're automatically on the right track. When must PDS be in place? The drop dead date is the In Service Date, for the simple reason that for the first six months all new equipment is 'blacklisted'; that is, subject to mandatory Narrative Fault Reporting and Investigation.

Crucially, the sole arbiter is the Technical Agency, not the project manager. They may be the same person, but only if he is an engineer with Technical & Financial Approval delegation. This excludes an increasing number of MoD's project managers, who should always have in mind who is going to be appointed Technical Agency, and make sure he is involved in every design and safety decision. It's money in the bank. They need to accept that the Technical Agency-elect is by far the more important role, with greater authority and responsibility. Nothing he does is 'by committee' He's named, and fully accountable. The last thing you need is a Technical Agency having to play catch-up at the last minute. Especially when non-technical project managers discover they are not permitted to make the appointment.

I mentioned Defence Standard 05-125/2. It is entitled *Post Design Services*, and was mandated in every aviation contract. Any incremental acquisition (or technology insertion) job must call up 05-125/2, because it is the only Standard that sets out the procedures. Let me be blunt. If you're managing this type of work, in any of its phases, and don't know 05-125/2 backwards, problems are inevitable. *So why has it been cancelled without replacement?* The proof is in the pudding. Today, the Red Arrows' Hawk doesn't have a valid Safety Case. Nimrod didn't. Chinook didn't. Hercules didn't...

PDS does not enhance; that requires a separately endorsed requirement. However, an enhancement may be conducted under the PDS contract, subject to a separate contract amendment. It does not procure, except to develop modifications; but resolves component unavailability. It does not produce modification sets or assemble kits; it carries out trial and proof installations on them. It does not repair faults, except on the Sample and Reference Systems; it investigates why faults occur and develops solutions. It prepares amendments to publications; it does not print or distribute them. In short, most of PDS is not volume-related. It costs roughly the same whether MoD has one, or one thousand, of a given equipment. Therefore, and like the integration work I discussed earlier, its funding must be kept quite separate, and ring-fenced.

In Service Support, and all upgrades, updates and follow-on buys, are predicated on the build standard being maintained. Only then can one have a valid Safety Case, set contractual baselines, and contemplate use. PDS having a separate grouping serves as a constant reminder that safety is non-negotiable. It is the means by which one mitigates the constant potential for harm.

Refusal to conduct PDS lies behind some of MoD's worst waste of life and money. Today, the definition used by the Military Aviation Authority (MAA) is completely wrong, and few in MoD can define it correctly. This is evident in the proceedings of almost every accident Inquiry and Inquest. None seem to appreciate that many of their recommendations amount to - *conduct PDS*.

As I said, it is wise to approach any new equipment project as a PDS task, and adapt. On a typical avionic PDS contract there will be scores at any one time, with hundreds on a major equipment. (Nimrod radar seldom had less than 300 on the go). It's the classic spinning plates scenario, suited to a certain type of person; one able to visualise the linkages between every task. Similar to 'basket weaving' but infinitely more complex and time-critical, so delegated as far as possible. PDS Tasks are projects in miniature, and one quickly learns to visualise the entire Cycle and appreciate context. It's not the size or cost of the task that's important, rather the sheer range of practical problems that arise and need solving. Quickly, because by definition all are safety related. In six months a Technical Agency gains more know-how, and makes more critical decisions, than many project managers ever do.

In my experience, this is the basic template for delivering to time, cost and performance. MoD may scoff, but it's been proven many times. If a project is in trouble, the first thing to do is check for compliance against 05-125/2. Similarly, most fatal aircraft accidents in the last 30 years would have been avoided by applying it. For example, Nimrod XV230, Chinook ZD576, Hercules XV179, Hawk XX177... Fifty-four dead in just those four. There was nothing wrong with MoD's technical and procedural 'system'. It was all about people. What did it do? Change the system, and promote those who refused to implement the mandate.

Burn the flames

A 28% reduction in PDS funding was imposed on 1 April 1991, while concurrently action was put in hand to transfer the Technical Agencies (all of whom at this time were also project managers) to AMSO; effected on 1 April 1992. At a stroke, MoD(PE) lost most of its 'cradle to grave' corporate knowledge and expertise. No sooner was transfer complete, than AMSO combined the financial pots and imposed further similar cuts for the next two financial years (to end 1993/94). Their view was PDS did not generate a 'due-in' on the Stock Computer (as maintaining safety is an intangible in this sense) so it was regarded as a waste of money - fatally flawed reasoning along the same lines as DM87.

Inevitably the successive cuts bit. Investigation of faults ceased. Amendments to technical publications were stopped. Drawing sets became out-of-date, meaning production would be delayed. Safety Cases became progressively invalid. Operational capability was degraded. The effect was immediately catastrophic. On 2 June 1994

Chinook ZD576 crashed on the Mull of Kintyre, killing all 29 on board. It was neither serviceable nor airworthy, and had no valid Safety Case.

In the RN, nowhere was this policy more apparent than the case of Lynx helicopters making heavy landings due to smoke in cockpits, caused by crumbling Bakelite terminal blocks associated with the aircraft power supplies to the radar. The words *'fire'* or *'smoke'* or *'fumes'* in an incident report is a drop everything moment. Designers go to extraordinary lengths to prevent such events, because if they occur an incident can quickly became a catastrophic accident. To a pilot, the time between detecting a fire, and landing, is the definition of eternity. Hence the unique financial delegation to the PDS Officer.

But with aircrew in sickbays, RAF <u>suppliers</u> refused to fund the <u>engineering</u> investigation or mitigate this serious, and immediate, risk to life. The RN could ground their fleet and come a-begging next year - a disregard for fire hazards that has resonance with the later Nimrod XV230 and Hercules XV179 cases. It was the ultimate advance warning of what would prompt the Nimrod Review 15 years later. The Technical Agency suspended a low priority RAF contract (Hoffman Lightweight TACAN), and used the funding to make Lynx safe. A few years later, under the new Integrated Project Team model, that degree of flexibility and authority no longer existed. But the really important question is this: *How many would have stood up to senior RAF supply officers in this way?*

Foxy Vixens

Blue Fox radar was fitted to Sea Harrier FRS1. Like other Fleet Air Arm front line radars (Sea Searcher in Sea King and Sea Spray in Lynx) the Falklands War in 1982 had disrupted development. Post-conflict improvements were limited to an interim 'Jamming Package' (better performance in jamming), and a longer Full Development phase for 'ILIC/AnderWave' (even better performance in jamming). This was essentially a Technology Demonstrator Programme for Blue Fox's replacement, Blue Vixen, and the Eurofighter (Typhoon) ECR90 radar; development of both commencing shortly after the war.

This sequence of events reveals scrutiny was carried out correctly. That Blue Fox was lacking some <u>desirable</u> features is not in doubt - this quickly became apparent in 1982. But it met its specification, written by MoD and endorsed by the RN, in full. The Jamming Package, a series of minor modifications, was quickly approved, as it could be argued on safety (self-protection) grounds. But the endorsement of Blue Vixen and ECR90 meant there could be no formal <u>upgrade</u>. ILIC/AnderWave was a risk reduction measure for future programmes. Many referred to it as a 'Mid-Life Upgrade', but the required timescale was only that it be ready for Blue Vixen. The final conversions took place the year before Blue Fox left service, meeting time, cost and performance criteria.

Today, former Sea Harrier pilots from that era complain about Blue Fox's alleged lack of performance. But none ask what the endorsed requirement was, and if it was met. A common phenomenon is mixing timelines up in hindsight. One doesn't belittle the Wright Brothers for not breaking the sound barrier. Fundamentally, their superiors had a choice to make. Upgrade Blue Fox, or get the world-beating Blue Vixen. They chose wisely. Contrast this with the AEW discussed later, where MoD has chosen to continually modify kit that was obsolescent when Guglielmo Marconi was an apprentice. Okay, I exaggerate for effect, but only slightly.

Any debate is ended by what happened when Vixen arrived. Foreign countries, <u>and the RAF</u>, were knocking on the project manager's door asking if they could have the remaining 53 sets of Blue Fox Mk2. Other countries, even India who had Blue Fox Mk1, weren't allowed it due to ILIC/AnderWave. The RAF wanted it for Tornado, to replace the Buccaneer role, but the airframe modification was too expensive. (The diameter of the radar yoke was too large). But another factor was at play. When the RAF Operational Requirements Branch offered its outline specification to Ferranti, the Chief Designer had a quick glance and said *'Blue Fox meets this'*. Initially excited, the penny soon dropped. *If the Navy are getting rid of something that meets the best spec we can think of, what on earth's replacing it?* Blue Vixen. (ECR90 also far exceeded what the RAF asked for). The matter was quietly forgotten. This served to highlight the disconnect in Main Building. One Service didn't know what another was doing. Scrutiny was taking place far too late; or not at all.

The only other endorsed enhancement to Blue Fox was an increase in operating altitude, requiring modification and requalification of power supplies. It might be thought there would be no arguments. But RAF suppliers had other ideas, seeing this as an opportunity to have another dip at Ferranti and the project office. A supply officer attended a design meeting in Edinburgh demanding to know how a modified power supply could be checked at 50,000 feet, given the aircraft was single-seat and an engineer was required to conduct the test. Which didn't go down well with the Managing Director, a retired senior RAF officer. The Chief Test Engineer's *'Using a bloody long cable'* seemed to suffice.

Back in London the development of Blue Vixen was being managed by a Group Captain. (By coincidence, the aforementioned former AMSO officer who did not support the *savings at the expense of safety* policy). He sought the Blue Fox project manager's advice on PDS costs, as the RN had not stated a requirement. *If you don't ask, you don't get*, but he sought to insert *some* funding. His financiers had agreed in principle, but were limited to the same level as Blue Fox, as the financial pot simply said 'Sea Harrier radar' instead of separate pots for FRS1 and FRS2/FA2. That seemingly innocuous error (by Main Building, who no longer had a Provisioning Authority to keep them right) ignored the 5-year rule, with Blue Fox funding (correctly) sitting at 20% of what it used to be.

Blue Fox had £xxk in that penultimate year; plus a one-off £xxxk for the Disposal task, which was not PDS funding but would be carried out as a PDS task. The project manager's advice was around £1.5M per year might be more appropriate for Vixen, given the complexity of the software and its new Software Support Facility. After some creative accounting the Vixen budget was bolstered, but insufficiently and at the expense of other projects.

Some years later precisely the same mistake was made on F-35B Lightning. Materiel and Financial Provisioning was to a great extent based on Sea Harrier experiences. But Lightning is a huge step-change in complexity, requiring significantly more resources to achieve the same output (in terms of flying hours), especially carrier operations.

There are a number of lessons here, the main one being you need a Provisioning Authority who 'owns' the equipment and is the Service's trouble-shooter. There's many a Group Captain who would have walked away saying *'RN's problem'*. Let's face it, the RN walked first. While the final Provisioning Authority had got it right in 1988, the RN's 'Shopping List' hadn't been updated as the design matured; and the single funding line error should have been picked up at scrutiny. *(Step #13)*.

Matters came to a head during Exercise REGEN in 1996, a largely paper exercise to determine if the RN could meet the Draft Naval Regeneration Plan. Flag Officer Naval Aviation (FONA) asked the Sea King project office to submit a paper explaining why vital avionic assets for Sea King, Lynx and Sea Harrier could not be located, or were unserviceable. All paths led to the Hallifax Savings (shutting down the Provisioning Authorities in 1988) and AMSO's *savings at the expense of safety* policy of 1987.[41] That FONA had to seek advice on Lynx and Sea Harrier from Sea King confirmed the effects of these policies, and the loss of corporate knowledge. It can be seen where cracks begin to develop. Sea Harrier funding was poor for the remainder of its life.

Forest for the trees

I've mentioned BOWMAN, the Tactical Communications project. Usually referred to as an 'Army' system, it was also due to be fitted to 13 aircraft platforms. By 1997 the plan was to save money by trialling it in just one of those, and *assume* it would then work in the rest. Anyone familiar with systems integration, or even building an Airfix model, will tell you this is absurd. A suggestion that BOWMAN recruit someone to manage aircraft integration was dismissed out of hand. The scale of the resultant waste can never be known.

While essentially the same BOWMAN radio would be used (the basis of the assumption), it was not understood that each platform needed a far more expensive secure intercom with the correct interfaces. In fact, so poor was the scrutiny and programmatic integration, that (e.g.) Chinook didn't even have a secure intercom. Yet other aircraft offices in the same Directorate had identified the requirement over a decade before, setting aside real estate for the BOWMAN kit and designing their existing systems to accept the technology insertion. When that occurs it doesn't take a genius to identify the point of breakdown - the first point of intersection in the management chain, some of his aircraft being to the correct specification, others not.

This all sounds complex, but is simply managed. When quantifying his requirement the Provisioning Authority is required to make provision for (in this case) a Comms System Integration Rig, held on the PDS contract at the System Coordinating Design Authority. In practice there need not be a complete rig for each configuration or platform. If, say, Chinook had decided to buy the same secure intercom as the RN (what expert RAF engineers wanted, and what had already be bought for Nimrod but not fitted), it was a routine task to create a multi-purpose rig. Plainly, BOWMAN scrutiny should have picked this up.

---

41 Loose Minute D/DHP 69/1/1, 10 July 1996.

128

Here, the system had worked the other way round, but only up to a point. The Technical Agency who controlled the rigs realised that BOWMAN had not asked for them to be reconfigured. *He* approached BOWMAN and together with the Design Authority gave them a presentation; but was shown the door. *No, our plan stands. We'll check our radio in one platform, and if the other 12 have difficulty, that's their problem.* They didn't say which lucky platform they'd selected, so *that* aircraft office would now be bidding for money it didn't need. To explain...

BOWMAN had ignored the 'agent of change' principle. That is, a huge £2.5Bn project was delivering equipment that would have an impact on other equipments and platforms; so had to make provision to resolve this by paying for design, modification sets, trials and installation. (Their strategy for land vehicles). Or, by agreement, ensure that the platforms did. They didn't; so belatedly the platforms had to try to find the money themselves - in effect, pulling BOWMAN out of the mire. (A cost never included in the £2.5Bn). By ignoring this basic requirement, expensive kit could not be put to its intended use. BOWMAN needed to accept their error, which is difficult when it's been the subject of purportedly rigorous scrutiny by committees.

'Intercom' may sound simple, but (e.g.) a Sea King ASaC Mk7 installation had 49 units, the biggest in the aircraft. The RAF's solution for Chinook and Hercules was to raid the RN's stores and 'acquire' Sea King and Lynx secure intercom and radios that had been placed in quarantine pending embodiment. Once again illustrating just how time, cost and performance is affected by not having a Service HQ postholder whose job it is to understand these issues, and make the correct materiel and financial provision. In the event, BOWMAN was many years late, giving the aircraft offices a little breathing space; but concealed the systemic nature of the failings.

Was this notified to the Defence Procurement Agency Executive Board? Yes, in a Post Project Evaluation Report sent to the Deputy Chief Executive, for lessons to be learnt. He took no action.[42]

Scrap metal

Integration Rigs are fundamental to attaining and maintaining functional safety. Any PDS task, upgrade or update is predicated on

---

42 ES(Air) 24/4/93 (D/DHP/24/4/93), May 2001. ECS Post Project Evaluation Report.

their existence, and them being maintained. On one project, the Design Authority was contracted to assemble and test complete aircraft installation sets on two separate rigs. This was to be witnessed and signed by the project manager and Aircraft Design Authority, the latter undertaking not to degrade the achieved performance when installed in the aircraft. But when the time came to commence work, Air Member Logistics (formerly AMSO) had dismantled the rigs, part of their *savings at the expense of safety* policy.

The Hovering Hercules Group Captain I mentioned earlier stated his position, and that of the RAF, very clearly. He demanded that Assistant Director Helicopter Projects 2 (AD/HP2, Kevin Thomas) report GEC-Marconi Secure Systems in Basildon to the police for theft of the rigs. Kevin thought him quite insane and ignored him.

Yet the Group Captain received support from his opposite number in the Aircraft Support Executive (Navy), a civil servant. You see, they had been *his* rigs, and many programmes were relying on access to them, which his predecessor had of course granted. Need I speculate as to why he wouldn't want this broadcast? Each rig cost nearly £1M. Three months slippage had to be recovered. (Overtime, mainly). And MoD had 73 contractors doing this work on avionics, most with multiple rigs.

Lightweights

I mentioned earlier the RN bought 'equivalent systems', and had 126 radars to fit and support an 82 aircraft fleet. Now let us look at when the RAF needed 150 to keep a fleet of 19 flying. And then ran out. I'll use the words of the *'Notes of a visit to RAF Finningley on 15 February 1989 to discuss support problems on ARI 5955 in Sea King HAR Mk3'*, issued as D/ARad 130/18/6 on 21 February 1989.

Background

Prior to 1982, ARI 5955 Light Weight Helicopter Radar was fitted to RN Wessex HAS Mk3 and Sea King HAS Mk1/2, and RAF HAR Mk3. Approximately 190 sets had been bought (150/40). The RN Maintenance Policy was 1st and 2nd Line at user units, 3rd Line at RNAY Fleetlands, with an additional 2nd Line Filter facility at RN Air Radio Workshops Copenacre. Equipment Beyond Unit Capability was sent to 4th Line, at MEL, Crawley. The RAF, however, only conduct 1st Line/Depth A at units/flights, relying entirely on the RN's Maintenance Policy and facilities.

The RN's use of Light Weight Radar decreased from 1982-onwards, as ARI 5991 Sea Searcher was introduced on conversion of Sea King HAS Mk2 to Mk5, and effectively ended in 1985. Four sets are retained for teaching purposes at HMS Daedalus, although on 25 September 1985 the Directorate of Naval Warfare (DNW) asked for 30 sets to be quarantined for future fit to Sea King HC Mk4 (one Maritime Counter Terrorism squadron). This will negate the need for the Mk4s to be accompanied by a Mk6.

Copenacre closed in 1983, and with it the dedicated Filter. The effect on the RN was nil, but the RAF had now lost 'their' only 2nd Line facility. Fleetlands' resources and manpower (one diagnostician and one fitter) were reallocated to Sea Searcher, with proportional arisings expected on Light Weight Radar. They were not tasked to provide a 2nd Line Filter, and the RAF declined to establish their own capability.

The problem

Financial provisioning for logistic support is based on the assumption that 80% of all arisings at 2nd Line will be recovered there (i.e. the Air Station bench, not a remote Filter bench), the remainder going to 3rd or 4th Line.

It follows that if the 2nd Line recovery rate drops (or in this case is non-existent), there will be a bottleneck at 3rd Line as they no longer have the resources to cope, and are not tasked to do so. Consequently, there will be a shortage at front line. In this case, the shortages have taken longer to manifest due to the high number of radars the RAF inherited from the RN. This transfer of ownership was formalised between DGA(N) HQ (PAE5) and the RAF in 1986. ('PAE5' was the Provisioning Authority).

Although around 150 systems remain in service, barely enough LRUs are available to fit the 14 operational Sea King HAR Mk3s. Fleetlands have been inundated with LRUs requiring, at most, minor repair or adjustment; the main bottleneck being the time to then re-qualify them, which requires the only test bench and all available manpower. There are no serviceable stocks.

Financial provision was cut proportionately when the radar became RAF-peculiar; but it has become apparent the resources necessary at 3rd Line to support the RAF fleet of 19 actually exceed that necessary to support the RN's 82. This is obviously a gross waste of money.

On 14 February 1989 RAF Support Command contacted the project office for advice and assistance, and a meeting was convened at RAF Finningley (SAR Force HQ) attended by the project office, Fleetlands' diagnostician, Finningley's Senior Observer/Instructor, a SNCO maintainer, and their Engineering

Department (AEDIT). The Design Authority, MEL, provided assistance remotely, primarily through replicating operations on the Reference System.

The principals convened in the stand-by aircraft on the pan, and then in the office of the Senior Observer.

The main concern raised by operators was perceived poor video gain of the system, meaning only very close targets were presented on the display. As there is no engineering training at all, the only perceived solution (by all RAF users) is to replace the entire radar (nine LRUs). Upon receipt and initial test at Fleetlands, the vast majority are fully serviceable; confirmed by MACE data from Swanton Morley.

Fleetlands asked that the Senior Observer demonstrate in the aircraft how he operated the radar. The local church spire was seen, a few hundred yards away, but no other targets. The Observer confirmed he would at this point snag the radar; and the avionics Flight Sergeant that he would remove all LRUs and fit a complete new set.

Fleetlands' diagnostician demonstrated operation of the Swept Gain control on the Control Radar Set, and targets up to 40nm away appeared. (The original specification called for detection of a Wessex at 20nm, with the aid of an Enhancement Transponder). The Observer confirmed that RAF practice was that aircrew should not touch these controls. It was explained that the ones they were not meant to touch were under a screwed-down flap, and locked in position with locknuts.

This confirmed that neither operators nor maintainers were being trained sufficiently - a significant finding with wider implications, especially given the world-wide deployment of RAF SAR Flights.

Conclusions, recommendations and actions

The root causes of this near-grounding of the RAF SAR fleet were failure to update the RAF Maintenance Policy upon closure of Copenacre, and lack of training.

The aim now is to achieve a situation whereby the 19-strong RAF SAR fleet (14 + reserve) can be supported within the laid down provisioning parameters. This will reduce the burden on Fleetlands from maintaining 150 radar sets, to around 40.

It was recommended that Finningley establish a 2nd Line bench, and to this end the RN Engineering School at Daedalus (Mr McNally) has been authorised to *transfer one of his four rigs to the Air Station, set it up, and conduct a training course. In parallel, AEDIT will undertake a review of the support policy with a view to formalising these actions. Similarly, the Senior Observer will update aircrew training. MEL will provide support to these activities.*

A further consideration, the maximum range and sector scan capability of the Fleetlands bench (given its new location) must be ameliorated, and to this end a task has been raised to relocate the Scanner onto the roof of the workshop.

DNW will be asked to re-confirm the HC Mk4 fit policy. Why these RN assets were removed from quarantine without DGA(N) approval, or informing DNW, is a separate matter.

Costs will be borne by the Rotary Wing Support Line (Fleetlands) and PDS contract at MEL, Crawley (MEL and Daedalus).

This example, and there were many to choose from, encompasses most of the issues I have discussed. Soon, the RN's Anti-Submarine Warfare and Search and Rescue fleets would also have suffered. Yet a few days work, at minimal cost, and the RAF's long-range SAR capability was resurrected and stabilised, and assets released for their intended use. The recurring savings were substantial. And one cannot put a price on the Search and Rescue fleet being fully available.

What made this possible? Applying Requirement Scrutiny rules and Defence Standard 05-125/2. How was the project manager able to succeed? Because he was also the Technical Agency, able to assume the role of RAF Provisioning Authority, and to commit RN and RAF resources. And a significant and beneficial aspect was the request for assistance came from RAF Support Command HQ, not AMSO. They cared not who cracked their problem, as long as it was, and showed their appreciation by awarding commendations. A cooperative approach, and perhaps the main lesson.

The good news? The diag and project manager were on free brandy all night, and dropped a hundred quid on the Officer's Mess bandit. The bad? Four years later AMSO threatened the same project manager with dismissal for doing precisely the same thing, on the same radar!

Group 7 - General

34. What stocks do we already hold at Depots, units or elsewhere, and what outstanding orders are there; i.e. orders from previous years?

35. For how long will there be a requirement?

36. What is the life of the store? If it is short, could it be lengthened and at what cost?

37. What is the current rate of usage and what is the projected rate of usage?

38. What is the War Maintenance Reserve?

39. Has industry the capacity to take on the work?

The supply manager can answer #34, and the first part of #37 by interrogating the supply computer. The Provisioning Authority will check if this is a true reflection of the actual requirement. The data informing #35, 36, 38, 39 and projected rate of usage is central to his role, and he must have it to hand for every aircraft type and every avionic equipment.

I've already covered the issues. But it will be clear these final questions are often the most ignored, yet they address crucial concepts such as remaining life, usage rates and War Reserve, forcing the scrutineer to think of wider issues and go over his previous answers. It is here that a deeper understanding of materiel and financial provisioning can be gained.

III

CASE STUDIES

Chinook HC Mk3

'The purchase of these helicopters is one of the most incompetent procurements of all time. Today, nearly seven years since they were delivered, the Chinook Mk3s are still languishing in climate-controlled hangers - despite the fact they are desperately needed on operations in Afghanistan'.

Edward Leigh MP, Committee of Public Accounts Chairman, upon publication of the National Audit Office report 'Chinook Mk3 Helicopters' on 4 June 2008.

I don't entirely agree with this. As I said, there's a huge difference between requirements and procurement failures, and this case is where it is most apparent. Both occurred, but only the procurers were blamed.

When this audit report was issued, the various committees had met many times to discuss Chinook Mk3. They carefully bounded their work to avoid Mk1 and Mk2, and barely mentioned the Mk2A. Without this context the true picture can never be seen.

Background

Chinook support problems were evident from the outset. In the early-80s a transmission repair facility was built at an MoD workshop, the first outside the US. The Instrument/Avionics Shop and Calibration Lab supervisor was tasked with commissioning the three new test rigs for the Fore, Aft and Combiner gearboxes.

The main difficulty was the Combiner rig trying to walk across the hangar, the whole building shaking. Everybody was standing outside, while he and a fitter ventured in. After wandering round the huge rig a number of times they eventually sussed it. A shut-off valve had been wire-locked closed, and the main pump was hammering against this blockage. Problem solved, on to the flowmeters. Wash, rinse, repeat.

The underlying failure was a recurrence. The same had happened not long before on the new 18-gallon pump and Blade Lag Damper rigs. In all cases the companies had been paid in full to deliver them, but their contracts didn't actually require them to prove they worked, or provide any support.

Those responsible said, *'What's the problem, you repaired it'*. But a repair isn't complete until verified, and no Rig Test Schedules had been supplied. The supervisor only *thought* them serviceable, but couldn't prove it. There was no audit trail. Chinooks tend to fall out of the sky if their gearboxes fail. In fact, the first to use the rigs in anger were the Air Accidents Investigation Branch, who were hanging around waiting to commence an investigation. A few years later, on 27 February 1987, seven RAF servicemen died in Chinook ZA721, victims of similar Quality Control and audit trail failures in the flight control system, with RAF Odiham denied the correct test equipment.[43] The warning signs had been there.

In August 1992, RAF Director of Flight Safety, Air Commodore Martin Abbott, declared to the RAF Chief Engineer and the Assistant Chief of the Air Staff:

'Boeing do not fully understand the contractual requirements to act as the Design Authority'. [44]

'The current organisational structure for tasking and fleet management, and the lack of resources, is not a healthy recipe for the future sound airworthiness of the Chinook'.[45]

He characterised Chinook as the *'Cinderella'* of the RAF's aircraft. In short, the Defence Lines of Development (in their previous guise, and for reasons explained) had collapsed. In the following six years he conducted a number of Airworthiness Reviews of front line aircraft, each more scathing than the last. The Chief Engineer, who in April 1994 became double-hatted as Air Member Logistics, clearly didn't like what he read, and the reports were neither circulated nor acted upon. Why? Because the root cause of the failings lay in the *savings at the expense of safety* and *DM87* policies. Which he was now responsible for.

Design control

In regulatory and procedural terms, Boeing had been <u>appointed</u> (not merely accredited) without undergoing the same rigorous assessment demanded of UK Design Authorities. Exacerbating this, the US Army acted as Design Authority for its own Chinooks. This highlights a

---

43 Chinook ZA721, 27 February 1987. Board of Inquiry Report.
44 'Chinook Support Authority Office Review', 20 March 1992, paragraph 6, reproduced *in toto* in the Chinook Airworthiness Review Team report (CHART), 2 August 1992.
45 CHART report, D/IFS(RAF)/125/JO/2/1, paragraph 1.

fundamental difference in approaches to design control. In UK parlance the US Army were merely the Design Custodian for their particular build standards, with at most a set of Secondary Master drawings that had to kept aligned with the Masters. Such a situation usually only occurs in the UK if the original designer no longer wishes to be Design Authority.

When the Director of Flight Safety said Boeing didn't *'fully understand'*, what he meant was they were unaccustomed to the day-to-day tasks required of, say, Westland, in the UK. Anyone in MoD with an aviation procurement background, transferring into Chinook, would be utterly confused at this, because it ran counter to Controller Aircraft's Instructions. The main bad habit they would learn is that, on Chinook, mandates and legal obligations were optional. Which is exactly what lay behind the Mull of Kintyre accident in 1994.

Specifically, Boeing could not *satisfactorily* undertake the 17 core components of maintaining the build standard; and in particular the common thread of Configuration Management. This remains the case. There are many official references to Boeing's poor performance in this respect, among them the Air Accidents Investigation Branch report into the aforementioned ZA721 accident. How, then, were Boeing accredited, and what evidence underpinned their appointment? What Standards did their contracts invoke? Where was the authority to waive mandates, and under what new procedures were Boeing and MoD staff acting?

What is the primary output of the contract that controls the design? A valid Safety Case, without which an aircraft cannot be declared airworthy. Yet the RAF had done just that. Little wonder the Director of Flight Safety's 1992 report was buried for nearly 20 years. But in response to a <u>member of the public</u> uncovering it, in 2012 MoD finally admitted that a major consideration was the government policy of not *'prejudicing relations between the UK and US Governments'.*[46] That is of no comfort whatsoever to bereaved families.

Chronology

In December 1980 the RAF took delivery of the first Chinook HC Mk1. 'HC Mk1' is the RAF designation. To Boeing the aircraft were basically CH-47Cs, with the RAF adding modifications. MoD is often criticised for

---

46 Defence Equipment & Support letter 22-12-2011-121642-005, 15 February 2012.

not simply buying US equipment off-the-shelf. But we don't always use our aircraft in the same way. Any deviation from the US specification or concept of use requires lengthy and expensive recertification. MoD's policy of preventing continuity in project offices means this corporate knowledge is routinely lost, gained again through mistakes, lost again...

In November 1990 a Full Authority Digital Engine Control (FADEC) for Chinook Mk1 was contracted to the engine supplier, Textron. The contracting route was convoluted, with the Safety Critical Software written by a sub-sub-sub-contractor, free of charge, meaning MoD had zero input or control. If you accept an offer to design and produce something free of charge, don't expect the supplier to be flexible or to tolerate interference. Boeing were not in the loop, and by 1992 had still not received any data on the system from MoD. This procurement strategy was a critical error, because MoD now carried the highest risks. Problems became inevitable.

Meanwhile, Boeing had significantly upgraded their CH-47C design, the new CH-47D having improved engines (but no UK FADEC), composite rotor blades, a redesigned cockpit to reduce pilot workload, enhanced electrical systems and avionics, and an advanced flight control system. Boeing were contracted to modify the Mk1 fleet, creating the Mk2. FADEC was delayed and a decision taken not to fit it to Mk1 but subsume it into the Mk2 upgrade. To Boeing, the Mk2 was not really a CH-47D. It was simply too different due to the major changes in design and aircraft handling. One practical issue arising from this was that MoD had to waive the normal requirement for a check flight before delivery to the UK. The Treasury Solicitor must approve acceptance of equipment off contract when it cannot be certified correctly. Did he?

The procurement strategy, and consequent delays, should have been a huge red flag. Point proven when, before FADEC testing could begin on a Mk2, the design was accepted in May 1993. Boscombe Down, who were required to verify the Safety Critical Software, could not; not least because MoD had failed to seek access to the source code. The policy directives covering this had been ignored.[47]

On 30 September 1993 Boscombe reported FADEC software implementation was *positively dangerous*, and MoD(PE)'s 3-Star

---

47 DUS(DP) letters 924/11/2/9, 31 December 1987 and 14 December 1989. 'Joint MoD(PE) / Industry Computing Policy for Military Operational Systems'.

Controller Aircraft mandated upon the RAF that the aircraft was *'not to be relied upon in any way whatsoever'*, and <u>must not</u> be released for Service regulated flying. [48] [49] The Assistant Chief of the Air Staff ignored him and falsely declared to aircrew that the Mk2 was airworthy.[50] The almost immediate effect was 29 killed in Chinook ZD576, the Air Accidents Investigation Branch confirming the *'positively dangerous'* status remained unchanged. Papers subsequently uncovered revealed that, for example, Air Officer Commanding-in-Chief Strike Command knew that the Mk2 was not airworthy, and why. This being so, it is inconceivable the Chief of the Air Staff did not know.

Chinook HC MK2A

In the meantime, in 1993 14 more aircraft were approved. Boeing had modernised their manufacturing techniques and the fuselage was now a milled structure, so these would be designated HC Mk2A. But the entire approvals process ignored that the Mk2A would inherit the same limitations, restrictions and risks that plagued Mk2; primarily, and the ultimate showstopper, it was not airworthy. How to deal with this technical, legal and contractual prerequisite? The regulations are clear. Instead, MoD chose to ignore them, and Boeing in Philadelphia were contracted in March 1995.

However, on 6 July 1995 a decision was made to split the buy into 6 x Mk2As and 8 x Mk3s; the latter for the Special Forces. Defence Procurement Minister James Arbuthnot approved this in his first day in post. The Public Accounts Committee later depicted this as being *'ambushed by people taking advantage of the new boy'*. It is the way the system works. New Ministers are keen to be seen to make their mark, and there is also the convention that they must not comment on the decisions of their predecessors. In practice, he was simply rubber-stamping a significant body of work that had already been given the nod by his two short-lived predecessors. Arbuthnot inherited a chaotic situation, and was quite definitely <u>not</u> told that the Mk2 was unairworthy. We know this because he later chaired the Mull of Kintyre Campaign Group, his

---

48 Boscombe Down letter AEN/58/119(H), 30 September 1993, and Report TM 2210, paragraphs 2 & 3, October 1993.

49 *Inter alia*, Boscombe Down Letter 001 TM2210, INTERIM CA Release, Task No. AENP 1536, CAR October 1993.

50 Mull of Kintyre Review, paragraph 2.2.8.

primary motivation being he had been lied to when Minister; only discovering much later, from the father of one of the deceased pilots, that MoD had been suing the engine manufacturers over defective FADEC software.

This is the point at which all committee reports mislead. They simply say that the Mk2As were delivered, entered service, and have operated successfully. Instead, they focus on the Mk3s; but it can be seen that in a fundamental sense - safety - they cannot be separated. The decision to make the split, and the way it was decided, was the primary root cause of what followed. Procurers were simply told to get on with it.

Chinook HC Mk3

The Mk3 was intended to be low-cost variant of the new CH-47E, with improved range, night vision sensors and navigation capability and made distinctive by having 'fat tanks' on the sides. But a bespoke variant is seldom 'low cost'. Once again, the same Mk2 limitations, restrictions and risks applied. That is, all Chinook work remained dependant on the outcome of the Mk1 FADEC contract. The Mk2A In Service Date was to be May 1998, but the conversion to Mk3, and additional certification work, meant this was changed for Mk3 to January 2002.

The 14 aircraft were built in Philadelphia with standard analog cockpits, then the eight intended to be Mk3s taken to Boeing in Shreveport and upgraded with a 'half-glass', or hybrid, cockpit (Multi-Function Displays for each pilot, with legacy analog instruments remaining in between). These were delivered by December 2001, Boeing meeting their contractual commitments.

But while accepted off-contract, MoD was unable to demonstrate the new hybrid cockpit met UK Defence Standards, as this had not been specified in the contract. Once again, it had not sought access to the Safety Critical Software source code, and it could not be verified by Boscombe; repeating the FADEC failure. Like the Mk2s in 1993, the Mk3s could not be proven airworthy.

The official explanation is that MoD had assumed that certification could be 'read across' from recently procured Netherlands aircraft; but *their* build standard was sufficiently different that this was impossible. The assumption had not been verified prior to contract award, meaning the cost estimates were low, and timescales optimistic.

Such a fundamental dependency would require a report from

Boscombe confirming the assumption. The dynamic between them and the rest of the MoD at this time must be understood. When the split procurement decision was made, in July 1995, their formal advice would be: *The Mk2 is not yet airworthy, so there is no valid baseline for Mk2A or Mk3.* To even suggest otherwise would contradict numerous <u>ongoing</u> formal reports by their Superintendent, who received his airworthiness delegation direct from the Chief of Defence Procurement. Again, this has never been discussed. But given Boscombe were being actively excluded from Mull of Kintyre inquiries, it is unlikely they were sent to the Netherlands to study the build standard and certification.

All committees have presented this software verification failure as a one-off. In fact, they knew it was a recurrence. They had complained about FADEC in previous reports, and were well aware that the problem was still ongoing when the Mk2A/Mk3 contracts were let; <u>and</u> when the aircraft were accepted off contract. The Mk3 could not be declared airworthy, but no committee mentioned that neither could the Mk2/2As. The reason for omitting this was to avoid the impact the truth would have on the Mull of Kintyre case. They were happy to criticise civil servants over procurement decisions, and even call for their sacking; but would not do the same to senior RAF officers who had committed imprisonable offences that lay at the root of 29 deaths.

'Fix to Field' and 'Reversion' (aka Back to the Future)

There is little in the record about the years 1998 to 2004. In fact, the background 'politics' were a repeat of 1993. Pressure was being applied on procurers to deliver; quickly, and within existing resources. A 'Fix to Field' plan was approved in September 2004, to cost a further £215M with a planned In Service Date of 2008; later revised to 2012.

But shortage of helicopters in Afghanistan prompted cancellation in March 2007. A new plan was devised, called 'Reversion', to revert the Mk3s back to what had originally been delivered by Philadelphia. This would not take so long, and an In Service Date of 2010 was predicted. The cost was to be £53M, instead of £215M, and was approved by the Investment Approvals Committee (IAC) in July 2007. Only then did discussions begin with Boeing, who quoted £105M. Once again, this suggests the procurers were being kept at arm's length. In November 2010 this was *'negotiated down'* to £90.1M; much of the difference explained by MoD contracting QinetiQ to convert the aircraft.

It is unclear why the IAC accepted the £53M estimate. Perhaps because what the committees claimed to be a *'robust'* business case was reviewed and accepted by the Office of Government Commerce, which had concluded that MoD *would* succeed in delivering the required capability. No committee has explored the reasoning behind this decision, what justification was offered, or what if any input they sought from procurers. In August 2007, five months after giving approval, the IAC chairman expressed disappointment at the level of evidence provided. So why did you approve it? Did you not see it failed scrutiny?

By mid-2008 the eight Mk3s, at the reverted build standard, were to cost £389.41M. However, the aircraft could only be given a limited Release to Service. They were not fit for their intended purpose, requiring a 'Night Enhancement Package'. Briefly, they could only fly on *'cloudless days'* below 500 feet. This has never been explained adequately, but 'cloudless days' is infinitely more restrictive than 'Visual Meteorological Conditions'. And lack of an 'enhancement package' should not preclude a Chinook flying in Instrument Meteorological Conditions or at night. This was a huge retrograde step as Mk1 and Mk2 had no such restriction. Due to these airworthiness issues, the aircraft were placed in storage at Boscombe Down, who were paid to maintain them.

Procurement issues

There were two primary failings.

First, the contract delivered an unairworthy prototype. That was inept, but one must also ask what possessed Boeing to accept it. Again we return to the rather strange relationship that exists between the company and MoD. The committees omitted that this repeated the Mk1>Mk2 conversion, where the aircraft were accepted off contract, and released to service, while Boscombe still didn't have a Mk2 on which to conduct testing and trials. Instead, they had an unrepresentative prototype. Why were no lessons learned?

Second, the same failure to acquire access to software code occurred on four consecutive Chinook projects (FADEC, Mk2, Mk2A, Mk3). Again, why were no lessons learned, despite constant representations from Boscombe? The Public Accounts Committee got very close to this on 18 June 2008, but asked the wrong question:

'Can you give us an indication of who stayed with the project all this time to make all these cock-ups or are folk constantly moving on?'

'No member of staff has worked continuously on the Chinook Mk3 procurement from its original approval in July 1995. Postings to the Chinook IPT, in common with postings across the Ministry of Defence, are normally between two and five years in length'.[51]

MoD's carefully worded reply was disingenuous; the IPT was only formed in 1999, and staff shared their time between all Chinook programmes. A better question might have revealed who retired from the RAF during the Mk1>Mk2 programme and immediately joined Boeing, and what influence they sought to bring to bear to protect the company's (and the RAF's) reputation; especially on Mull of Kintyre. One was an Air Ranking officer and former RAF Director of Aircraft Engineering. And at least one civilian engineering project manager stayed with Chinook for over 20 years, and was still there in March 2010. That is not to say he did anything untoward - quite the opposite - but why was the anti-corruption rule being applied so strictly to others relaxed for him? For over 18 years. A rhetorical question. He knew the truth and had to be kept close.

The first question asked of these staff should be: *Did you point out that the baseline aircraft was not yet airworthy?* It is unimaginable that someone (in addition to Boscombe) did not record this as the #1 risk on Mk2A and Mk3. Having made the decision to evade the issue, the RAF and senior procurers were welded together between a rock and a hard place. It was either admit to serious offences, or plough ahead with Mk3 knowing it <u>would</u> be delayed. Against Boscombe's advice, they chose the latter. *Who benefitted?* One need only ask who was controlling the Chinook agenda.

Projects are not permitted to proceed until a certainty has been mitigated to an acceptable risk. That is, the problem, and the way out of it, must be understood. Here, the main certainty was that the Mk2 was not airworthy to UK standards. While the project office (and Boscombe) knew what had to be done, a major hurdle was pressure from the RAF; themselves under pressure from the Army (who fund Chinook) to deliver troop lift. And even if viable, the time taken to implement any mitigation plan had to be added to the front end of the project plan. Delays were a certainty. Quite how the requirement passed scrutiny

---

51 Public Accounts Committee report: Ministry of Defence: Chinook Mk3, 9 February 2009.

defies all reason, when the basic question could not be answered: *What is the design and safety baseline?* It was so fundamentally flawed, it should never have been offered for scrutiny.

And overshadowing everything else, mid-way between approval and contract award, Chinook ZD576 crashed. Everything related to Chinook was then driven by the perceived need to lie about cause, and blame the deceased pilots. It is also important to appreciate what was going on in the wider Directorate General. Regarding Safety Cases, once again precisely the same error was made on Nimrod. The MR2's wasn't valid and the aircraft wasn't airworthy, making delays to MRA4 a dead certainty.

Personnel issues

The committees asked a number of times that MoD identify the individual who managed Mk3 and made the decision not to seek access to the source code. MoD replied that it didn't know; and that in any case the decisions were made by committee. If I may...

In late-1993 a decision was made by the RAF that only RAF officers would manage RAF helicopter projects. I know this because in early August I was selected after interview to manage the new Sea King HAR Mk3A (Search and Rescue), but upon taking up post on 3 December was told of the policy by a very unhappy Director, Dr David Hughes, who was most apologetic. At that time the 2-Star Director General was Air Vice Marshal Peter Norriss, which we thought significant. I was instead given a newly formed avionics section. The same happened again in late 1994. Dr Hughes appointed me project manager for this buy of 14 Chinook Mk2As, but on the morning I was to take up post was told the RAF had insisted a Wing Commander be appointed. Neither officer was ever told they were not the Director's choice.

But matters had changed dramatically by the time we were moved to Bristol in July 1996. Most obviously, there was a young fast-tracker doing the job. That is, he had skipped the first five grades, would serve a period at the sixth, and grade-skip to the eighth. His notional boss was an outstanding Squadron Leader who had been the Chinook Engineering Authority; above him the Wing Commander; and then the new Assistant Director, Colonel Barry Hodgkiss. The Air Vice Marshal had been replaced by a civilian, Mr Ian Fauset. It became all too apparent that the fast-tracker was under the personal mentorship of Mr

Fauset. This peculiar situation meant everyone in-between had to leave him to get on with it, as they were not privy to what directives (if any) Fauset was issuing.

But the Squadron Leader, who had his own projects to manage, was appalled at the decisions being made, especially on avionics and software. He would ask project managers on other aircraft to have a word. To a man they were told in no uncertain terms to butt out, as he was mentored by the Director General. Everyone in the Directorate knew who was running Mk3 and making the decisions.

I have no evidence of the decision-making process, only the end results; but the above narrows matters down considerably. However, I was one of those asked to have a word, on the navigation system. The Squadron Leader and I were left speechless by the intention to ignore the mandate that GPS cannot be used as the primary navigation aid. (The Air Accidents Investigation Branch had pointed out the same thing at the Mull of Kintyre Fatal Accident Inquiry only a few months before). Our advice was that such a concept could never be certified, and the proposed design would waste precious funding and cause delay. I would like to think Boeing said the same. But that single event meant what transpired on Mk3 came as no surprise to me.

When he left shortly after this, to become DGAS2's assistant in a newly created post, his replacement (an experienced engineer) essentially had to start again. To be clear: when *he* took over he was not responsible for any delay. This was someone who knew what he was doing, picking up the pieces and doing what should have been done all along.

As a sub-plot, the project office had a team of civilian engineers who worked alongside the RAF Support Authority team in Philadelphia. A dozen or so staff in total. The main bone of contention, to both the project office and Boeing, was the RAF's persistent use of Service Modifications and Special Trials Fits (STF), which were not (and could not be) appraised against a stable build standard, and so were not included in any Safety Case. For example, on the day of the Mull of Kintyre accident the Chinook HC Mk1 had 39 STFs. There was no indication in the (falsified) Mk2 Master Airworthiness Reference that any had been superseded, yet many remained. That would need to be resolved before any follow-on contract could be contemplated.

(This STF issue reached its zenith with Tornado, where the tri-national arrangements meant that the RAF could not use Service Modifications. They used STFs instead - in 2001 there were around 650 active STFs on the Tornado fleet. Once again, the main violation is that there is no appraisal to ensure the airworthiness certification remains valid. A prime example arose on Tornado F3, where one STF had the effect of disabling the Infra-red flare dispensers).

What did the procurers in London think of all this? It is known that Colonel Hodgkiss' predecessor, Captain Mike Brougham RN, expressed grave concerns over safety aspects on Mk2, and was supported by Dr Hughes. By definition, these also applied to Mk2A and Mk3. Two of Brougham's memos, dated 29 April 1994 and 11 January 1995, were quoted by the House of Commons Defence Committee in 1998. He was clearly laying down markers. *When this turns to rats, here's your starting point.* He acted entirely correctly; again narrowing matters down.

Costs

The contract for 14 Mk2As was to have cost £129M, around £9.2M each. But including avionics they were £12.63M. (Which sounds quite cheap, but Chinook is not well appointed). To that must be added the engines, supplied separately by MoD at £2.63M per aircraft. (Placing MoD at risk through being responsible for the performance of FADEC, repeating Mk1 and Mk2). To place this in some sort of context, Sea King was at the same time committing ~£25M to upgrading each AEW Mk2.

The Mk3s eventually cost £48.68M each, but much of the contract value was non-recurring costs due to the unique design. In other words, if more had been bought, that £48.68M would be greatly reduced.

Once again the committees deceived, failing to compare like with like; implying the cost had increased by over £39M each. (£9.2M to £48.68M). At no point did they make an assessment of the *fair and reasonable* cost - but nor did the RAF.

Boscombe Down

An important yet unmentioned aspect is that Boscombe's software assessment section was tiny. Their most critical task across all Air Systems was FADEC. They knew it must take precedence over Mk3, because it was a technical and safety prerequisite. This is utterly crucial.

Only Boscombe acted correctly throughout. Contracted to verify

FADEC software, they had been provided the hardware tools to carry out Static Code Analysis. But, to the Defence Committee in 1999 and 2000, Defence Procurement Minister Baroness Symons (among others) criticised them for wanting to conduct Static Code Analysis. She omitted they were under mandate to. This lie was only revealed when explained to the Mull of Kintyre Review in 2010, helping make Lord Philip's decision to exonerate the pilots easy. But matters were compartmentalised, no committee told this applied equally to M2A/Mk3. And even if able to access the source code, there could be no guarantee it would be written in a way which might make it comprehensible for analysis purposes. These facts, and they are fully documented and incontrovertible, put matters in a quite different light.

The Mk3s languished in storage at Boscombe Down for some years. The committees thought this the worst possible outcome, not realising it was the path of least pain. If the same rules had been applied elsewhere, the Mk1/2/2A fleets would have been sitting beside them.

To summarise Boscombe's position on FADEC at the time of Mk2A approval, and Mk2A/Mk3 contract award:[52]

'Although only 17% of the code has been analysed, 21 category one and 153 category two anomalies have been revealed. One of these, the reliance on an undocumented and unproved feature of the processor, is considered to be <u>positively dangerous</u>.

This density of anomalies (code and documents) is large; one category one and three category two would be more reasonable. Worse, the nature of the software is such that corrective action is considered to be impractical, and independent verification is virtually impossible. The assessment has been abandoned, rather than completed, on the grounds that the software is of <u>proven inadequacy</u>. The results are in fact similar to those derived from a study of the development standard which was terminated in September 1990 for similar reasons'.

After confirming that *'some of the* (software) *versions tested are not even direct ancestors of the current versions'*, and disqualifying the testing conducted on these older systems, they concluded:

- *The density of deficiencies is so high that the software is unintelligible.*
- *Because of the density of deficiencies, it would be impractical to maintain the*

---

52 Letter AEN/58/119(H), 30 September 1993. 'Chinook Mk2 - T55 Engine FADEC Software' from Superintendent Engineering Systems.

software as re-verification of all the software would be required after every change.

- *No assurance can be given concerning the fidelity of the software, hence the pilot's control of the engine(s) through FADEC cannot be assured.*

- *The standard of engineering is demonstrably not that expected of software intended for the purpose of controlling a safety critical function in the aircraft.*

- *Although it is never possible to quantify the risk associated with the use of software, in this case it is obvious that available measures to ensure the quality of engineering for safety critical software were not employed.*

- *Controller Aircraft Release for Chinook Mk2 with this version of software in FADEC cannot be recommended.* (Hence the mandate from Controller Aircraft that the Mk2 could not be relied upon in any way whatsoever).

This was finally corrected in 2010, over 20 years after FADEC was let, with the introduction of a new Digital Electronic Control Unit (hosting the software) as part of an upgrade to a new engine. It had a new Central Processing Unit, the basis of the *'positively dangerous'* statement.

I have one question for you. *Does this sound like a mature design that could be used as a baseline for Mk2A and Mk3?*

Summary

Recurring failures are always the worst, not least because the aim of any safety management system is to avoid them. All the failings here were recurring, in effect handing an open-ended contract to Boeing. Requirement Scrutiny was non-existent. The procurement strategy breached all known protocols and instructions. Having had over two years to think about the requirement, the RAF's decision (or was it the Army's?) to completely change it three months after contract award invited failure. The inability to appreciate one had to start again on the Lines of Development transcended incompetence. This also applies to the Investment Approvals Committee and MoD(PE) Executive Board; who, it must never be forgotten, were concurrently making the same mistakes on Nimrod MRA4. And would again on Apache. And then BOWMAN. And then... And the same management handed the task to one of their most inexperienced staff, with his four immediate line managers effectively excluded; exacerbated by the MoD/Government's supine appeasement of Boeing and the US Government.

But let me play Devil's advocate for a minute. If a Chinook project manager had said to me, *'The Mk2 baseline only stabilised to the Independent Safety Assurer's satisfaction in 2010 (i.e. the new processor), so by definition Mk3 could not be certified before that'*, I'd have to agree. I wouldn't have been happy at the requirements decisions, but actually they weren't on the critical path.

Gliding Into Extinction

With grateful acknowledgments to Commander Steve George RN
(Retired)

In 1984 the RAF found itself in possession of a significant underspend. It decided to replace the ageing wood and canvas Slingsby gliders used by the Air Cadet Volunteer Gliding Squadrons (VGS); purchasing, off-the-shelf from Grob Aviation, a German firm:

- 81 Grob 103 two-seat gliders (named 'Viking T.1' in RAF service).
- Approximately 50 Grob 109b Motorgliders ('Vigilant T.1'), plus a further 'opportunity buy' of 15.

The Air Cadet Organisation was to manage gliding. This was largely run by volunteers, whose skills were not assessed in the same way as servicemen and MoD's civilian engineers. To replace Mobile Glider Servicing Parties, a Central Glider Maintenance Flight was established at RAF Syerston, in Nottinghamshire. A maintenance contract was awarded to SERCO; to replace RAF staff, who were deemed unable to maintain the Glass Reinforced Plastic Gliders - which probably came as some surprise to MoD's experts at its workshops. The Glass Fibre Bay at Syerston was run by Soaring Oxford Ltd, to repair Vikings. Planned service life for the Viking was 26 years (to 2010), 24 years for Vigilant.

The RAF now operated the world's largest fleet of composite gliders, but contracting out their maintenance was a new concept. There was no UK-based Design Authority, and Grob did not have the necessary UK approvals. Instead, the RAF contracted Slingsby Aviation Ltd (SAL) to act as the 'Designated Aircraft Design Organisation'. But that is only an accreditation. It doesn't mean they are a competent Design Authority, which is a formal appointment. In 2010 SAL were bought out, and are now part of Marshall Slingsby Advanced Composites.

Such windfalls have to be spent in-year, so the acquisition was rushed and corners cut. Never mind, the RAF now had a veritable empire. But with no effective Design Authority, and no in-house expertise, to what Standards were they being maintained? To this day no-one can say.

Between 1984 and 2014, airworthiness and serviceability of the gliders was largely ignored. Across Defence aviation standards slipped and mandated regulations were ignored, yet formal declarations made by senior officers that they were being adhered to. Few noticed or cared, and by January 1993 the RAF's policy to run down airworthiness had succeeded. The contractual vehicle to control repair standards, DefCon 112(Repair), had fallen into disuse, the RAF's supply organisation unhappy at the authority it vested in engineers. Meanwhile, the RAF had designed and installed a number of modifications to both types, despite Boscombe's warnings of limited margins for growth in All Up Weight.

Moreover, while each Volunteer Gliding School had a Volunteer Reserve 'Technical Officer', this was far below the standards required on 'regular' RAF aircraft, where each air station had an entire engineering hierarchy headed by a Wing Commander. Nor is it clear who held airworthiness delegation or inspection approvals at each level. (MoD will grant airworthiness delegation, and permits self-delegation, without first attaining inspection approvals. The latter requires the passing of formal examinations; the former does not, and is based on rank, not competence).

A cardinal error had been made. TheDefence Lines of Development had been ignored.

Structural audits in 2002 (Viking) and 2009 (Vigilant), carried out by QinetiQ, sounded alarm bells. Both were epic failures. For example:

- The remaining life of aircraft was not accurately known.
- Fundamental material properties used in the construction of both types were not fully understood or substantiated.
- A large number of aircraft were damaged beyond repair, some broken up for spares.
- The aircraft were operated without a Safety Case. There was no legal authority for them to fly.
- The status of design, static and fatigue type records were *'unknown'*. The Vigilant audit, especially, could not be completed until this was resolved, and there is no indication it ever was. As a result, instead of being flown as powered gliders, they were now flown as normal powered aircraft.

To explain this last... Vigilant was procured as a self-launching glider; avoiding the need for winch launches, so allow gliding to take place at a wider range of airfields. The intent was to shut down the engine when at the desired height, and the aircraft would then be flown as a glider. It could be restarted for the landing, or for a climb back up to gliding height. Alas, this proved unreliable, with frequent failures; so the RAF used the engine continuously. The mandated update to the Safety Case couldn't take place, as there wasn't one.

The declining state of the fleet was revealed in rapidly falling flying hours. Cadets were travelling long distances at week-ends, and being sent home without being able to fly. Seemingly, no-one drew the links to root causes, such as: poor engineering practices, lack of due diligence, unauthorised modifications, and unauthorised repairs. MoD's policy of compartmentalisation meant that the same failures being revealed concurrently on, for example, Hawk, and managed by the same part of MoD, were concealed.

Between 2010 and 2014 the RAF carried out four reorganisations of the gliding organisation. But once again no-one considered the risks or impact on safety, despite the Nimrod Review having reiterated in 2009 the effect of this *organisational chaos* on airworthiness management.

By 2012 planning for the future was taking place, and a substantial strategy paper was produced for Air Officer Commanding 22 (Training) Group, setting out a vision for Air Cadet gliding. Key points were:

- The Out of Service Dates had moved to 2025. No reason was given.
- Some damaged Viking airframes had been sold off to civil clubs for repair and recertification as civil aircraft. Others had been broken for spares. Oddly, and without explanation or justification, the paper said all these aircraft could be recovered.
- There was no endorsed output for the Air Cadet flying task. A staggering admission. The RAF had been throwing money at the glider fleet, and blindly accepting whatever it did or didn't produce.
- It was recommended that a new fleet of 54 motor gliders be sourced, or an 'output based' contract be let to deliver 16,000 flying hours a year.

It went unsaid that the aircraft were unairworthy, as this would have exposed a number of senior officers and officials to legal action. It is unclear if the same people endorsed the paper's recommendations.

2012? What was going on at this time, in precisely the same part of MoD? The investigation into the death of Red Arrows pilot Sean Cunningham, killed in November 2011 in an unairworthy, unserviceable, and unfit for purpose aircraft. The only question should have been: *Will the sentences run consecutively or concurrently?*

Two further Continuing Airworthiness audits took place in 2012 and 2013, under the auspices of the Military Aviation Authority (MAA). Both were spectacular failures. The audit team looking at No.2 Flying Training School (2FTS) swiftly called a halt, not even getting so far as looking at any actual aircraft documents. The highlights included:

- 2FTS was not in control of all aspects of Continuing Airworthiness. (That is, of individual aircraft, not the Type).
- 2FTS could not ensure that qualified personnel were working on the aircraft.
- Fault reporting was not being properly managed.
- Quality Assurance was ineffective.
- Independent auditing of contracted glider servicing had not been carried out.
- 2FTS was unable to identify the Configuration Status Report, an essential building block of airworthiness.
- There was a lack of maintenance programme analysis (checking that the maintenance being carried out was working).

The MAA's report concluded:

'The organisation lacks maturity and the oversight and control required for the issue of an approval... The MoD Continuing Airworthiness Manager must respond to these findings with a Corrective Action Plan or closure within 28 days from release of this report... MAA approval of 22 Group Glider CAMO will not be issued until all findings have been closed or a MAA agreed Corrective Action Plan is in place'.

The statement that the organisation *'lacks maturity'* hides the point that senior staff, sitting above the MAA, had declared that it *was* mature, and that they had confirmed this through regular audit. The report omitted any assessment of when the situation had changed from (alleged) maturity, to immaturity, why, and under whose direction. The reader might be excused for thinking this had only been a requirement since the MAA had formed in 2010.

Worse, it was omitted that the failures permeated MoD's Air Systems, and so was systemic. Precisely the same had been noted by the Nimrod

Review in 2009; which led to the formation of the MAA, whose job it was to correct it. *They* were now marking their own homework, so one can only imagine what else their report omitted. It was implied these were relatively minor and easily fixed local errors; when in fact MoD had permitted those responsible to sign legally binding declarations that the work *had* been carried out.

This was damning stuff, and utterly pejorative. Notably, AOC 22 (Training) Group between July 2007 and April 2009 became Director General of the MAA in May 2013. These audits of his old command were carried out in his name. Did I mention marking one's own homework?

2FTS's authorisation to look after its own aircraft was withdrawn. There can be no greater indictment of a maintenance or flying organisation. Glider flying was 'paused' at the end of April 2014, a euphemism for grounding. But, once again, MoD didn't mention <u>precisely the same</u> failures had occurred in the Red Arrows, under the <u>same</u> AOC 22 (Training) Group. *Their* authorisation was not withdrawn, allowed to continue operating without a valid Safety Case. They still do.

Over the next 21 months, to September 2015, Officer Commanding 2FTS attempted to get the aircraft back in the air. The 'problem' was deemed to be with paperwork. The 'solution' was to seek more manpower to write-up this paperwork. From the outset it would appear no-one within the organisation appreciated how serious the problem actually was. The Officer Commanding had spoken, and he must be right. Right?

But, slowly, through public postings on aviation forums, acceptance grew, and it was realised that aircraft had been damaged by neglect and error - around 18 seriously. The Officer Commanding, a Group Captain, issued a series of statements about recovering the aircraft, but they were increasingly divorced from reality. A variety of plans came and went, none succeeding. The grounding became the longest experienced by any UK military aircraft.

After 19 months, just four of 146 aircraft were back in the air. In the meantime, 2FTS had not even identified root causes. Nor had the MAA (or perhaps it could not bring itself to criticise the new boss), who now directed the Group Captain to get his act together. What was really needed was for the MAA to get *their* act together. That is, implement the recommendations of the Nimrod Review, which in turn reiterated (without acknowledgement) the recommendations of a series of RAF Directors of Flight Safety, commencing August 1992. In turn repeating recommendations by MoD engineers from January 1988.

By now it was clear gliders were being selected as the scapegoat for long-standing systemic failings. No-one asked why far worse examples were being swept under the carpet. Or how other platforms had avoided the problems. (Answer - implement mandated regulations).

The following month, October 2015, Chief of the Air Staff (CAS) Air Chief Marshal Sir Andrew Pulford took personal charge, rejecting OC 2FTS's recovery plan. This intervention was well received, but entirely missed the point that it was not just an RAF problem, but affected all Air Systems. Pulford, of all people, knew this. He had been President of the Chinook ZD576 Board of Inquiry (Mull of Kintyre 1994), and knew precisely the same failures were still occurring - 21 years later. Nevertheless, he told OC 2FTS to come up with another plan, but *within available budgets*.

However, it is very difficult for a Group Captain, even if he understands the issues, to reply recommending that CAS's staff who, since 1984, had declared the glider fleets airworthy knowing they were not, should be stood down and never allowed to make an aviation related decision again. Also, that the regulatory authority, the MAA, should be roundly ignored in favour of mandated regulations and good engineering practice, and the *available budget* used instead to meet legal obligations.

Nonetheless, by taking charge Pulford showed he couldn't trust the MAA to do its job. And why would he? In 1995 his conclusion that the Chinook pilots were not negligent had been rejected by the then Chief of the Air Staff, Air Chief Marshal Sir Michael Graydon, who declared them negligent to a gross degree - the equivalent of manslaughter. Since its formation in April 2010 the MAA had actively supported Graydon, briefing against *anyone*, serviceman, civilian or politician, who dared support Pulford. In August 2011 he was mostly vindicated, the findings of gross negligence quashed by the Defence Council. They have yet to be replaced with an alternative finding.

In December 2015 an Initial CAMO Approval Audit took place. 2FTS failed again, on an astonishing scale. There were now 25 'Level 2' findings, which had to be cleared before approval could be granted.

There had been no progress, the audit comprehensively demolishing 2FTS's engineering organisation; and, by extension, 22 (Training) Group (including the Red Arrows) and all who claimed there was nothing wrong.

Once again the 2FTS and 22 (Training) Group response was a snow job. Determined to get the MAA off their backs, a Corrective Action Plan was issued. However, on examination it was a classic piece of staff work prepared to *just get something out the door*. Every one of the 25 separate responses within the plan, prepared on the MAA approved forms, was a cut and paste of the same old story, namely:

- Root Cause - lack of resources.
- Corrective Action - additional resource being sought.
- Preventative action - a *'core CAMO team'* had now been established and further additional resource sought.

So: *We didn't have enough people, but now we've asked for more, so happy days are here again.* But what of the Defence Lines of Development? Once again they had broken down entirely - if they had ever been erected in the first place. What of the multiple failures of Requirement Scrutiny? But apparently nobody had failed in their duty, not even those who had claimed valid Safety Cases existed. Systematic violations of heroic proportions were disregarded.

The MAA finally granted 'Initial' approval in June 2016. 2FTS and 22 (Training) Group could now, allegedly, do what they were meant to be doing all along. There was no mention of why they had been allowed to continue 'managing' their other aircraft during this hiatus. One could, it was said, point to there being no fatalities in that time. But that soon changed, Corporal Jon Bayliss killed in March 2018 as a result of the same old violations.

'Accidental' deaths had become manslaughter.

Meanwhile, the RAF embarked on a public relations offensive aimed at disguising the true extent of the scandal. It lied to Ministers, who misled Parliament. The *loss* of airworthiness became *'airworthiness concerns'*. It was announced 40% of the total glider fleet would be discarded.

The Chief of the Air Staff himself then went public, admitting to an *'exasperating period of technical challenges'* and *'safety issues with our gliders'*. Once again it was implied this was a revelation. Most significantly, he stated that *'...it was simply not an option to continue to operate without a Safety Case in place'*. He didn't say why they were operating without one in the first place, why other aircraft were allowed to, or why successive Assistant Chiefs of the Air Staff had made legally binding declarations that there was one. Nor did he mention the internal conflicts caused by the MAA issuing new regulations that could <u>not</u> assure airworthiness, while cancelling those that, if implemented, did.

Notably, the MAA's disagreement with Pulford continued. In a January 2018 interview, an MAA accident investigator characterised as *'rubbish'* the suggestion that airworthiness certification must be underpinned by a valid Safety Case.[53]

Armed Forces Minister Julian Brazier then became party to the cover up; although probably unwittingly as he was briefed by the Air Staff. His replies to MPs who were asking awkward questions obscured the full extent of the problem:

- He admitted only to *'an erosion of confidence in airworthiness'*. No Minister, the RAF had flown schoolchildren in aircraft it knew to be unairworthy.
- He talked of *'configuration control discrepancies'*. Did he understand this was a fundamental breakdown of airworthiness?
- He admitted essential aircraft documentation had been destroyed, omitting that three years previously the Hawk Deputy Type Airworthiness Authority, in the same project team managing gliders, had been unable to find *any* maintenance records in RAF archives.

Minister seemed not to appreciate that he had just listed serial failures of the Defence Lines of Development and Requirement Scrutiny processes.

In 2016 the RAF finally conceded it was unable to fix the Vigilant powered gliders. The latest plan was to hand over all 65, plus spare parts such as engines, to Grob, from whom they'd been bought in the first place. For nothing. Gratis. Not a bean.

In return, Grob would re-engine 15 of them and give them back to the RAF after a basic servicing. This was to be funded through a Department

---

53 'Red 5' (David Hill, 2019).

of Transport grant, conveniently distancing MoD from the entire saga.

But even if successful, these aircraft would only have two years life left before the declared Out of Service Date. The other 50 were to be reconditioned, for Grob to sell and profit from. Who could authorise such a hand out? The Treasury Solicitor. Was he even approached?

In May 2018 the RAF conceded more failure. The *'innovative proposal'* to get 15 Vigilants to run through to 2019 had failed. Officer Commanding 2FTS announced the 2016 proposal was *'no longer an option'*, and grounded the six remaining Vigilants. But failure of a 'proposal' is no reason for a grounding. There must have been a safety issue for the abrupt directive. So, 18 months into a 'recovery programme' for 15 Vigilants, the RAF had none in the air. The Air Training Corps was now left with just 48 Vikings. Only around 10 flew each weekend. Air Cadet throughput at Gliding Schools was now just over 5% of what it was in 2013, pre-grounding.

It was time to call in the MoD Police and Fraud Unit.

F-35B Lightning II ZM152, 17 November 2021

On 17 November 2021 an RAF F-35B Lightning II, ZM152, ditched whilst attempting to launch from HMS Queen Elizabeth. The ship was operating in the eastern Mediterranean, off the north coast of Egypt. As the aircraft left the end of the flight deck ramp, the pilot ejected and (only just) landed back on the deck. The aircraft impacted the sea and sank. The pilot suffered minor injuries and later returned to flying.[54]

This section looks at a few of the Service Inquiry's recommendations, and if they would have been necessary had previous recommendations been heeded. These reports make recommendations to 'enhance Defence Safety', tending to look only at the final act; so very often omit underlying factors or root causes. Here, the first was:

'Deputy Commander Capability should resource the Lightning engineering workforce at an establishment that delivers sufficient Direct Maintainer Spaces per Aircraft, increasing for embarked operations... to ensure enough engineers are available to deliver the task safely'.

Lack of engineers and pressure of workload meant an Intake Blank, used to prevent Foreign Object Damage to the engine when the aircraft is parked, was left *in situ*. The engine could not develop sufficient power. There was no proper way of securing the blanks or attaching them to each other. Nor was there proper control of them as sets once returned to the hangar storage.

The ship being short-handed meant the engineer had to work solo on the flight deck, with no *'defined procedures'*. Similarly, the required engineering standards could not be achieved because there were no procedures allowing for the concept of not using white light on the flight deck at night, meaning the Intake Blank was difficult to see.

The immediate response to the accident was disorganised, the Panel recommending that Flying Control Emergency Procedures be updated and reformatted:

'To ensure that users can easily find the relevant procedures in order to respond promptly to aviation emergencies'.

This missed the point that adequate training must be provided so that

---

54 Service Inquiry report, paragraph 1.3.1.

first responders do not need to refer to procedures.

A number of the issues identified had arisen before, for example in the aftermath of loss of two Sea Kings off HMS Ark Royal in 2003. The following were familiar to anyone conversant with both accidents:

'Implement a process for quarantining data in a timely manner... in order to preserve evidence for subsequent investigation'.

'Ensure that all weapons and countermeasures... have supporting orders that detail loading procedures, training, and assurance to ensure squadrons are fully prepared to employ them'.

'Ensure safety reporting is shared... in order to identify trends to minimise the risk of repeated incidents'.

'Implement a system that ensures that all quality assurance recommendations are addressed'.

'Provide clear guidance to aircrew and survival equipment technicians on the correct selection, fitment, and use of (safety equipment)'.

In other words, known risks and hazards had not been mitigated - a long-standing organisational violation, noted in almost every accident report released by MoD. It had been the entire thrust of the Nimrod Review.

The overall impression is, just as in 2003, there was a haste to be seen to operate the new aircraft off a carrier. In 2003 the Sea Kings were declared operational, yet still formally in their Training and Familiarisation Phase, with the crews not permitted to rely on the new Mission System or the navigation system in any way whatsoever - a contradiction in terms that was conveniently ignored by all three Investigations and the Coroner's Inquest. Precisely the same occurred in the 1994 Chinook ZD576 accident.

The F-35B itself may have been sufficiently mature, but the Support aspects most definitely were not. The Aircraft Safety Case may have been valid, but very clearly the Air System Safety Case was not. (The report mentions neither, an astonishing omission in any accident report to the Safety Authority). But MoD's way is to compartmentalise. The 2003 accident was to Sea Kings operating off Invincible Class carriers. In 2021 it was F-35B off Queen Elizabeth Class. *How can they be similar? Nothing to see here. Move along now.*

A root cause here was the gapping of capability, much as the gapping of Airborne Early Warning cost us dear in 1982. The grown-ups, who had stripped the Royal Navy bare, forgot that one needs to continually practice hard won skills, lest they fade. But in April 2000 the RN had ceded control of Harrier operations to Joint Force Harrier, an RAF-centric organisation. Carrier operations ceased in 2005, and Sea Harrier was retired in March 2006. Yet it was only in that year the UK announced its firm intention to acquire the F-35B. The first aircraft were delivered to RAF Marham in June 2018, and first operated off a carrier in June 2020. MoD talks correctly of 'skill fade'. The key argument for retaining Sea Harrier was not so much that the aircraft was needed, but skills needed to be retained. They weren't just gapped. They were obliterated, and will take many years to resurrect. You reap what you sow.

The Service Inquiry took 21 months to report. It did not mention the Defence Lines of Development, but it is clear that all eight Lines broke down completely. Once again, its recommendations to Director General Defence Safety Authority (DSA) can be summarised: *Do what you're meant to be doing.*

The DSA insists it is 'independent' of MoD (refuted by the Senior Coroner for North Wales in November 2021), with the Director General enjoying direct access to Ministers. That being so, one hopes he received an interim report within days, knocked on Minister's door and said: *'We can't do what you want us to do without resources. This time we got away without fatalities, but a £100M aircraft is at the bottom of the oggin'.*

The UK Military Flying Training System (MFTS)

Today's fast jet pilots are taking over seven years to be trained, double that planned. As I write, the new Chief of the Air Staff, professional head of the RAF, is being questioned by the Defence Committee. He's inherited a difficult position. His predecessor was told four years ago by the Secretary of State for Defence, Ben Wallace MP, that this was his #1 priority. Instead, he concentrated on ensuring everyone else was given priority over white males during selection. In evidence to the Committee on 2 November 2022, Wallace said:

'I am concerned that... we have gone backwards from when I gave my instruction to the Chief of the Air Staff. I do not think that is acceptable'.

I don't want to regurgitate the various committee reports. Instead, I want to discuss a root cause that the committees didn't mention. But first, a little background...

In June 2008, after a 2-year competition, Ascent Flight Services, a joint venture between Lockheed-Martin and VT Group (now Babcock International), were awarded an intricate 25-year 'training partner service contract', funded under a Private Finance Initiative (PFI). (Names have changed - I'll use 'Ascent'). MFTS takes students through elementary, basic and advanced training phases, before being posted to their assigned squadrons.

The high-profile failures have occurred in fast jet pilot training. There, elementary training is provided in Grob Prefect T.1s at RAF Cranwell and nearby RAF Barkston Heath; basic training in Beechcraft Texan T.1 at RAF Valley on Anglesey; and advanced training in Hawk T.2, also at Valley. The pilots then go on to fly Typhoon and/or F-35B.

MoD's MFTS Delivery Team is grouped into three teams:

- MFTS Programme Team, responsible for overseeing the management and delivery of MFTS.
- Hawk Delivery Team, responsible for the delivery of Hawk T.1 (Red Arrows) and Hawk T.2 for MFTS.
- Gliders Delivery Team, for RAF Air Cadets.

Contractually, the Directorate of Flying Training of 22 Group RAF is the user, Defence Equipment & Support (DE&S) the customer. The Type Airworthiness Authority for each aircraft sits in DE&S.

At time of MFTS approval the same people but under a different name were responsible for three aircraft types (Hawk T.1, Vigilant and Viking) that, on MoD's admission, did not have valid Safety Cases and had not been maintained to acceptable standards. That failure should have been their 2-Star's #1 risk; and mitigating it the #1 prerequisite to them being allowed to take on MFTS, whose success would depend on the team fulfilling its side of a complex contractual bargain. These ongoing violations were a clue something worse might happen, and could offer little confidence for the future. If one cannot understand these basics, then there is little chance of more multifaceted issues being managed correctly. It is only a case of *when* the system will fall apart.

The basic premise was that MFTS would save £1Bn over the 25 year contract. Since the advent of PFI similar claims have invariably proven mistaken, often based on optimistic assumptions as to what MoD will bring to the table.

This is called Government Furnished Information, Equipment, Facilities and Services, or GFX. It is what it says. When responding, bidders must include a proposed GFX Annex, which is scrutinised and agreed by the owners, invariably the Service. It is not unusual for a project to have thousands of items of GFX. The terms of the loan (Embodiment, Contract, Ordinary, Repayment) are then agreed. Only upon agreement can the contract be finally priced, yet it is rare indeed that the GFX Annex is finalised before contract award. It simply takes too long; and of course the contract price changes and timescale is at risk if the owner doesn't deliver.

In 1997 matters became difficult, for two reasons:

1. Air Member Logistics' Finance & Secretariat issued new GFX rules. Despite not owning or controlling the GFX, and without discussing their intent with the owners or MoD(PE), they took it upon themselves to dictate what companies would be allowed. This caused immediate delays and financial uncertainty. It was DM87 all over again. But at least they accepted the concept of GFX...

2. The Chief of Defence Procurement (CDP) issued an edict that in future no contracts were to have GFX. No modification programmes. No upgrades. Service HQs withdrew support from

many projects, project managers immediately facing demands that everything be bought new. This led to further delays and cost increases, CDP confirming he was content.

In neither case were guidelines issued, and extant regulations were not rescinded. So, while the MFTS contract turned out to be weak, before criticising anyone it would be wise to consider the position its staff were placed in by MoD's conflicting policies.

It can be seen GFX is a major risk, owned by MoD, and must be resourced accordingly. It is not, the immediate problem being the now defunct Provisioning Authorities are meant to manage this. The task defaults to an unprepared project office, who do not have the authority to agree the disposition of Service assets.

Contractors' negotiation teams tend to be very good, looking to probe for weaknesses. If these can be identified and exploited within the terms of the contract, MoD's primary aim (to transfer risk to industry) can be reversed. The GFX Annex provides the first opportunity. If MoD does not apply itself, and simply agrees to the Annex without understanding the implications, then that is not the company's fault. It is part of the cut and thrust of negotiation. The one certainty is that MoD will default at some point on GFX, and a good GFX Manager at the company will know where. On an aircraft upgrade programme, for example, he will immediately concentrate on the Induction Build Standard, because he knows MoD's policies militate against it delivering what is agreed. The first blank cheque is handed to him on a plate.

On MFTS the contract said MoD would provide Qualified Flying Instructors (QFI), a prerequisite to carrying out any instructional training. Ascent set about building the infrastructure to support their side of the contract, and in time said: *Right, send us the QFIs, we're ready to begin.* But MoD sent 'ordinary' pilots for Ascent to train as QFIs, which wasn't in the contract. MoD was in default, and the ability to deliver the very first batch of trained pilots was immediately compromised. And as each new course of students arrived, the continuity of the previous and late-running courses was jeopardised.

Each item in the GFX Annex must be linked to a requirement in the Tender; which either didn't spell out the QFI issue properly, or wasn't translated correctly into the Contract. It's no good *implying* something.

The company will only answer the exam question. It's in their own best interests. If Ascent had included the cost of training QFIs, their bid may have drifted above that of a competitor. And as I noted earlier, at this time companies were being effectively blacklisted by DE&S's Commercial Director for pointing out such omissions.

This is where 'partnering' arrangements fall down. All very well on paper, but Ascent are a business and there to make a profit. MoD is not but acts as if it is. MFTS was presented as a 'saving' of £1Bn, and the tendency in MoD is to immediately 'take' that saving. The practical effect is that the project office finds itself with less staff and resources; and if the savings don't materialise, front line suffers detriment. The uninitiated think: *It's being privatised, MoD has nothing to do*. In fact it is often busier, and in areas that are unfamiliar to the project office.

Who was MoD's GFX Manager? Given CDP wouldn't allow other teams one, with project managers told to provide assurances no-one was doing the work, did MFTS even have one? But if by chance there *was* an appointee, ask him this: *Were you provided with resources and support, both from your superiors and the GFX owners?*

Assuming for a moment there was one, he quite definitely had no control over the system which produces QFIs, never mind the wherewithal to increase their numbers. Before the contract was let he was required to seek written assurance from the Directorate of Equipment Capability (DEC) that *they* would provide QFIs. At the time, DEC's Requirement Manager sat in the Integrated Project Teams. He should have been the GFX Manager (as the primary 'owner'), but it is unlikely anyone in MFTS understood this. Either way, both he and his Main Building colleagues would have a copy of the GFX Annex, with their responsibilities clearly highlighted.

If there was no positive reply from DEC, one way or the other, then there was a Requirement Scrutiny failure (in that an original assumption was no longer valid). It was the responsibility of the MFTS team leader to escalate the risk to the Executive Board; and in any case the job of individual 2-Stars on the Board to assess the top 10 risks in each programme every month. Surely an inability to train pilots, in a £6Bn pilot training programme, was in the top 10?

The staff constructing the MFTS contract didn't consciously place MoD in default. *'Provide QFI's'* was perhaps buried in the proposed Annex between two innocuous items - an old industry trick. Long before reaching this page the person tasked with the job, by now brain dead, overwhelmed, and up against teams of company experts, may have taken to simply ticking the box. Did he even know what a QFI was? Nevertheless, the project office copy of the Annex (a database) must have contact details for each owner, and their stated agreement to provide the item. To compile this the GFX Manager must have intimate knowledge of all the GFX and the owner organisations. It needs someone very experienced with a certain background. But it's a soul-destroying task and far too many look upon it as a glorified clerical job. If the work has to be done by the project office, by definition the postholder is doing tasks well below his pay grade.

But the root failure on MFTS is this. A complete breakdown of all eight Defence Lines of Development. *Who initiates that process? Who (mis)managed that process?*

Airborne Early Warning (AEW) The Falklands War in the South Atlantic confirmed a known gap in capability, absence of an effective AEW capability to get inside the enemy's decision cycle. As the new Invincible Class carriers lacked catapults or arrestor gear, only a helicopter could be considered. In May 1982, while hostilities were ongoing, Westland converted two Sea King HAS Mk2s to undertake the AEW role.

The radar, Searchwater LAST (Low Altitude Surveillance Task), was an adaptation of Searchwater in Nimrod. This had been suggested in 1979 by manufacturer Thorn-EMI, after the Fairey Gannet AEW Mk3 was withdrawn from service. Belatedly, MoD agreed. The concept was proven, and eight more were converted. Various modifications were then embodied, including a second Observer position. In August 1985 a FIN1110 Inertial Navigation System and radar G8 Autotrack Computer enhancement were approved. Further minor changes followed, and in the late-80s development of a colour display upgrade commenced. Low radar transmitter power (and hence range) was recognised, and a high-power design undertaken in 1990 as a private venture by Thorn-EMI Varian, with MoD oversight at the company's invitation.

Airborne Surveillance and Control (ASaC) In 1992 a Radar System Upgrade (RSU) was endorsed. Essentially, this was the consolidation of these relatively minor tasks, coupled with better processing to handle the resultant increase in targets. So far so good, but in addition a number of technical prerequisite projects were endorsed separately. Without them, RSU would have no real benefit. The most significant were secure communications, Joint Tactical Information Distribution System (JTIDS), (another) new Inertial Navigation System (Ring Laser Gyro with embedded GPS), and Mode 4 Combined Interrogator Transponder IFF. Those that could be competed as a package were consolidated into a *project* termed Mission System Upgrade.

The true winner was an adaptation of the Ferranti Blue Vixen radar used in Sea Harrier FA2. The aircraft was to be Merlin. But a political overrule directed that the contract be let on Racal Radar Defence Systems, who hadn't bid. Sea King was to be retained, and LAST modified again. Racal then amalgamated with Thorn-EMI, and were later acquired by Thales;

who, as Thompson-CSF had withdrawn from the competition in 1995. One can perhaps appreciate the risks that were beyond the procurers' control. The original 10 plus a further three were upgraded to ASaC Mk7, entering service commencing 2002.

Future Organic Airborne Early Warning (FOAEW) ASaC was to have been an interim measure, witness the RN's refusal to convert newer, surplus, Sea King HAS Mk6 airframes built in the late-80s/early-90s. It insisted on keeping the (10) old Mk2s, which had all been original Mk1s from the late-60s. The plan was to retain and update the Mission System (Radar, JTIDS, Man Machine Interface), and fit it in Merlin. It was overlooked that the new Video Graphic Recorders, RLG/GPS and IFF would also transfer, and Merlin comms would have to be upgraded.

Concept work began while ASaC was in development. The obvious thing was to have, at the very least, a team in the same Directorate repeat their success. But the job wasn't even given to the same Directorate General. It was to be carried out by the Carrier Vessel Future team, who eventually delivered the new Queen Elizabeth Class carriers.

Expressions of interest were sought from industry in February 2000, and in 2001 it was announced the production contract was planned for 2006, with a 2012 In Service Date; a longer gestation than ASaC. Having announced 2012, ASaC funding would start reducing in 2008. That is, by 20% in each of the final five years. Contradicting this, John Spellar MP, Minister of State for the Armed Forces stated: *'There are currently no plans to withdraw the Sea King Airborne Early Warning aircraft from service'*. This was at total variance with the assumption that Merlin would be used, and caused consternation and confusion in MoD and industry. At this point, the scribes will tell you, delay heaped upon delay for over two decades. But the truth is more nuanced.

BAe/Northrop Grumman and Thales were contracted to conduct studies into future threats, and the defences needed. Thales were then contracted to submit two proposed system configurations, with a final one in June 2001; just as ASaC radar trials were getting under way in earnest. Their proposal was an Active Electronically Scanned Array (AESA) radar, in Merlin; contradicting Spellar. In many ways this was similar to the winning Ferranti bid from 1993, and was recognisable as such to anyone familiar with that period. It offered a flexible, future-proof solution which could simultaneously perform the vital functions of air, surface and land surveillance, and airspace, tactical air control and attack coordination. But for the political overrule on ASaC, it and FOAEW would have already been on the AESA development path. There was now an unbridgeable disconnect between AEW/ASaC and FOAEW, not of the procurers' making.

Maritime Airborne Surveillance and Control (MASC) At around the same time the RN was lobbying for the AEW Mk7 to be re-designated ASaC (too late to avoid significant cost), FOAEW was rebadged as MASC. A new name meant a new baseline. 'MASC is on time', ignoring that FOAEW had spent years going nowhere despite having ASaC as a template. MASC remained in the carrier team. In late 2000 they advertised a number of posts. This made the ASaC technical staff twitch. *It* was by far the more complex programme, managed by one full-time and two part-time technical staff. MASC was to have an entire team, with the team leader more senior than his ASaC opposite number. But with the ASaC engineers being actively stood down, MASC was an obvious move.

During interview in December 2000, one asked what assumptions underpinned MASC. He was horrified to learn the old FOAEW misconceptions persisted. It was a *'simple case'*, he was told, of transferring the ASaC Mission System, in its entirety, over to Merlin. Nothing more, nothing less. He replied saying this was technically impossible, the most basic reason being the Mission System Consoles were part of the Sea King superstructure. They couldn't simply be 'removed'; and even if somehow cut out intact, they wouldn't fit in Merlin (and the Sea Kings would need major repairs). A complete redesign of the aircraft installation was necessary, it being long held by the AEW and ASaC teams that a palletised solution would be best. He also questioned the intention not to upgrade the existing Merlin avionics, and ASaC-peculiar avionics. It was clear FOAEW/MASC hadn't spoken to Westland in any detail, or looked at the 1993 bids. ASaC staff were duly rejected on the grounds their *'AEW and ASaC experience is of no relevance to MASC'*. In other words, *We don't want you, you'll raise the bar.*

In April 2002 Northrop Grumman and Thales received another contract, for MASC Phase II. The Assessment Phase started in 2005. By the following year another three study contracts had been awarded, one each to Lockheed Martin, Thales, and Agusta-Westland. In 2007 the Osprey V22 AEW resurfaced as the amusingly named TOSS, Tactical Organic Sensor System. But not as good as the Weapons Tactical Fighter

General Overview (WTFGO, or *What The ****'s Going On*) function in ASaC Mk7. And what about the delicately named Trialling Wire Antenna Test Set. But none topped the good old Sea Harrier Intensive Trainer, because it was.

CROWSNEST In 2015, and with Sea King soldiering on with reduced funding, the requirement was rebadged yet again. A Demonstration and Manufacturing contract to the value of £250M was let on Lockheed, who were to run a competition. (That is, carry out a routine MoD task). They were one of the bidders, to themselves, along with Thales. (The cost differential - less than half - reveals CROWSNEST is minor compared to ASaC Mk7).

The 'winning' bid, by Thales (!), correctly ditched the plan to simply transfer to Merlin. But their proposal, naturally, was to retain and upgrade the ASaC Mission System. This has become convoluted, and I'll stop soon. But the upshot was:

- Lockheed lost, despite them being the prime contractor (suggesting political influences again).
- CROWSNEST will be a repackaged upgrade, not the new Elta EL/M 2052 AESA radar offered by Lockheed to... Lockheed.
- It is to be a palletised *(quelle surprise!)* role fit for the existing Merlin HM2 helicopters. There will be no permanent CROWSNEST fleet.

This last is problematic. The Merlin Anti-Submarine Warfare (ASW) fleet of 30 is too small to suddenly contribute 10 aircraft to CROWSNEST. A couple of unexpected minor events requiring deeper maintenance will affect the ASW fleet disproportionately. Put another way, the RN does not have the necessary Reserve aircraft. It didn't when AEW Mk2 and ASaC Mk7, which became all too evident when the two Mk7s were lost in 2003. Yet again, no lessons have been learnt. Of the 10, and after training and repair pool aircraft are taken into account, it is entirely possible the maximum available will be four or five. It is unclear where the figure came from. It is significant and, I think, not entirely coincidental, that the original AEW Mk2 and ASaC Mk7 quantities were also 10, against an actual requirement of 16. There is another potential reason. That, there is no intention to deploy the two new carriers at the same time. Only then does 10 make sense.

Initial Operating Capability was declared in mid-2023. But only two aircraft will be on the carrier when she sails, insufficient to fulfil her role.

Like the ASaC Mk7 in 2003, CROWSNEST will be in its Training and Familiarisation phase. That Initial Operating Capability is in reality very limited indeed. It has taken almost 30 years to get to this point, and it is unclear if anyone involved realises that the 'solution' is in many ways a retrograde step from what won the 1993/4 competition.

Two questions need to be answered:

1. How could this happen when the ASaC Mk7 was delivered to time and cost?

2. How did FOAEW/MASC/CROWSNEST pass scrutiny at any point in those 30 years?

Both questions relate to the fundamental issues this book addresses. The answers are unpalatable to MoD, because they would naturally expose inconvenient truths.

I do understand this section is slightly difficult to follow, but is typical of many MoD projects that undergo continual resets. (And I haven't mentioned the airship - dirigible balloon - and unmanned proposals of the late-80s, which MoD took quite seriously and may yet return to).

The primary reason for the successful transition from AEW to ASaC lay in continuity. The ASaC *programme* manager had long experience of AEW and wider RN aircraft/avionic projects, and of the three main contractors. The most obvious manifestation was risk reduction and prerequisite contracts being up and running within days, immediately stabilising the *programme* - although luck was involved as he hadn't been subject to the anti-corruption rule I mentioned.

But that continuity was broken with the decision to have the Carrier office manage FOAEW and MASC. They were treated as new stand-alone projects, despite the basic premise being to re-use and upgrade ASaC's Mission System - which is the technical heart of all five iterations. At the most basic level the next step was a modification, and should have been structured as such. The only decision to make was whether to have a single team, two sitting beside each other.

Even then, FOAEW/MASC could have benefitted had it not rejected the AEW/ASaC team members as being inexperienced in... AEW/ASaC. That was not a strategic decision, nor even a Personnel decision. It was an inexplicable decision made by one man, who chose not to explain himself. He denied himself MoD's entire procurement corporate knowledge. The result can be seen in the number of wheels reinvented in the following 20 years. Contractors and the RN will have been tearing their hair out for all that time, wondering why CROWSNEST, a lesser project by far, has taken so long. It is at least 10 years late (and arguably nearly 20). Regardless of whether it actually works or not, it must be seen as a failure. It is not the technical solution the Services wanted or need, and it would seem what they'll get is once again based on political geographics.

Nimrod

The cancellation and public scrapping of the Nimrod MRA4 fleet of maritime patrol aircraft in 2011 is often held up as an example of *procurement* incompetence. Over £4Bn was wasted.

The facts are very different, and easily explained. The Nimrod MR2 from which it was created wasn't airworthy. You couldn't help but know this. It just wasn't MoD policy, and the RAF's Director of Flight Safety had, for years, been banging his head against the walls of the RAF Chief Engineer and Air Staff. A known risk, in fact a certainty, had not been mitigated. MRA4 was doomed from the off.

Incredibly, the government finally conceded this on 3 February 2014, confirming the aircraft *'would never fly, would never be certified, and would never be able to deliver a capability'*. This (perhaps inadvertent) admission, by Secretary of State for Defence Philip Hammond, drew no comment from committees or auditors, and the media still will not publish what really happened. History has been rewritten to conceal the truth.

A fleet of airworthy MR2s was, contractually, Government Furnished Equipment. They would be fed-in with a Configuration Baseline of 'General Assembly Drawing, Issue 26, January 1996'. But no-one could define 'Issue 26', not even British Aerospace, the Aircraft Design Authority at Chadderton.[55] From the outset the contract had no known, never mind stable, baseline. Configuration Control is a fundamental component of airworthiness. Lacking it, one cannot with any confidence declare an aircraft safe. This is why, during the Nimrod XV230 Inquest in May 2008, Coroner Andrew Walker confirmed the MR2 *'was never airworthy'*. MoD did not demur because, as a matter of policy, it could not prove otherwise. It later emerged that MRA4 was finally built to 2007 drawings - an 11-year gap in the MRA4 audit trail. As the MR2 design was Under Ministry Control, this was MoD's liability.

The decision to scrap was made on 24 October 2010. The government and MoD claimed it arose from that year's Strategic Defence and Security Review. No-one joined the dots to the Nimrod Review; which

---

55 In November 1999 British Aerospace became BAe Systems.

had reported on 28 October 2009 and reiterated in piercing detail that MR2 was not airworthy. The Review took evidence revealing this was a result of the *savings at the expense of safety* policy. It agreed; although, as I've explained, dissembled about the start date.

As with Chinook Mk3, MoD claimed to committees that the matter was too complex, and no individual or group of individuals could be identified as culpable. This ignored concepts such as organisational charts, Directorate Management Plans, telephone directories; and that a *'tamper proof'* database holding this precise information had been created by the Directorate of Procurement Policy.

I always look for linkages that bind cases together. From an Air Member Supply and Organisation (RAF) letter of 6 July 1993:

'The introduction of New Management Strategy and the creation of Multi-Disciplinary Groups has put <u>Support Staff in control of the procurement process</u>'[56]

These support staff didn't claim to <u>do</u> procurement. They <u>controlled</u> it. AMSO had become Air Member Logistics in 1994. That placed them in control because they were responsible for delivering an airworthy MR2. If they didn't then the project was dead in the water. They exercised that control. It died.

You may be asking how this could be missed. Or, if it is fair to expect it to be picked up. I discussed earlier the scoping of projects. On an aircraft upgrade programme the <u>very first</u> thing you look at, and check the validity of, is the current Master Airworthiness Reference and the associated Safety Case Report. They tell you what you're being given to work with, and spell out the residual risks. DEC's first requirement in an upgrade programme must be to clear Limitations. That is, areas of non-compliance that the Service has agreed can be <u>temporarily</u> worked around; which, by definition, are all safety-related. As the project manager has no authority to carry over a Limitation into a new Mark, it is incumbent upon the Air Staff and DEC to ensure the project approval clearly states what they will or will not accept.

Nimrod MR2 didn't have a valid Safety Case or Master Airworthiness Reference. An immediate showstopper. But MoD ploughed on.

---

56 Letter D/DDSM8(RAF)/PRU/4/41/11, 6 July 1993.

I've discussed the need to have the right people. What was needed at this early point was someone to give it straight to the Executive Board:

I can do what you want and modify Nimrod, but my successors will never be able to certify it.

Even British Aerospace knew this, recommending to MoD that a new Nimrod production line be established to modern-day standards. But the contract was let, the known and insurmountable certainties stuck in a bottom drawer for the next poor sod. And so on, each incumbent but the last knowing they wouldn't have to make the real decision. And lo and behold, when that time came the person with the guts to make the correct decision was the one criticised. Retired senior officers bleated to the press. Nobody mentioned their contributions or culpability. The MoD line remains: *It was taken as a savings measure.* No it wasn't, and unless you know and admit the real reason you cannot prevent recurrence. So MoD just carries on wasting more money and lives.

What *should* have happened? Simple. Given the known status of Nimrod MR2, retaining and modifying it should not have been an option, and a new platform stipulated. The clue people already knew this lies in the original project name - *Replacement* Maritime Patrol Aircraft (RMPA). This changed to Nimrod 2000, and then Nimrod MRA4; each 'reset' providing a new start-date, shortening the apparent delay and hiding the root failure. Upon being told to modify MR2 the Project Director should have declared planning blight. This, I'm afraid, is where I've been a little repetitive, because the solution was:

Implement mandated regulations, and do what you're meant to be doing.

The procurers' Executive Board uses the term 'anchor milestones' to describe their approach to oversight. It identifies two or three a year on each major programme, and seeks a report confirming they've been met. Plainly, demonstrably, year after year they weren't. And, as I said before, individual 2-Star members are required to assess the top 10 risks every month, so would have immediate notice if an anchor was at risk.

In 2003 the Defence Procurement Minister, Lord Bach, told the Defence Committee a 4-year 'pause' in production had been ordered after the third (of, at that time, 18) aircraft had been built. He did not say, and probably didn't know, that five years before a similar delay had been announced internally. Although I did not work on Nimrod MR2 or MRA4, I happened to be present on 27 February 1998 when the

Director General was informed of this by an RAF officer, and he showed no surprise or concern. In fact, his response *('it's on schedule')* revealed he'd already accepted a revised In Service Date. Whatever, the reasons were the same - immaturity of design. MRA4 had entered production before known technical risks had been designed out. Such overlap is permitted, based on engineering judgment; but rather obviously too much overlap will lead to false optimism. *We've built x platforms. Yes, but is the design safe?*

My belief is that the pressure brought about by the first delay meant an uninformed decision was taken to proceed at risk. But the finger was pointed at British Aerospace; it being left unsaid that a key anchor milestone would have been the Production Readiness Review (PRR), which is what it says. Only by passing that may you seek permission to enter the production phase. But an unairworthy aircraft cannot pass any Configuration Milestone Review. This is important. Hitherto, who was a major player in the decision to transition to production? The Provisioning Authority, as he prepared the Board Submission seeking approval; and it would be subject to rigorous Requirement Scrutiny. Lord Bach was not asked, and did not volunteer, what process (if any) was followed when making this decision.

The programme didn't know where it was going, because it didn't know where it was coming from or where it had been. If the decision to go ahead doesn't work out (and it didn't), there is no way of knowing where to regress to. MoD's risk management was non-existent. Put another way, it persistently prioritises manufacture over verification. When this happens, regression becomes ever more costly. (This also applies to AJAX - see next section - where nearly 70% of vehicles were built and paid for while the basic design was non-compliant).

I should say here that a process called 'Earned Value Management' was taking root in MoD from about 2001, replacing traditional milestones. Suffice to say, it offered no confidence that Configuration Milestones were being met. If this was used on Nimrod, then the Executive Board would have been given a false sense of security. I'm being overly kind as any engineer would realise this, but it is only fair I point it out.

Quite the worst aspect is that this repeated the Chinook Mk1>Mk2 debacle of a decade before, when an alleged production standard Mk2 was delivered to Boscombe Down for assessment, only for them to label it an immature *'prototype'*. The Executive Board couldn't help but know this, as the main item on their agenda was the ongoing Mull of Kintyre case. Both aircraft had the same 2-Star Director General.

Astoundingly, in 2003 the Defence Committee let slip a reason why parts of MoD were secretly pleased at this further delay:

'MoD hopes that the pause after the third aircraft is delivered might provide an opportunity to enhance *the Nimrod design to be an "adaptable aircraft". The aircraft might be capable of deep-strike and network-enabling roles, in addition to its originally planned maritime surveillance and attack roles. The MoD envisages a possibility that the fourth and subsequent aircraft could have the "new adaptable standard" needed for any such wider capabilities'.*[57]

With this statement Nimrod MRA4 was, for all practical purposes, officially dead. It now failed so many of the *39 Steps* it's easier to say which ones it passed. It would have to be resubmitted to the Investment Approvals Committee. To be raised by the Defence Committee in 2003 meant this was in planning for some time, even years. Taken in the round, only an idiot would think the programme could survive. Once again, the Project Director was obliged to declare blight. Within his project office chaos would reign, but one fact is certain. That single paragraph by the Defence Committee should have been be sufficient to prevent any further MRA4 expenditure. But, while the Executive Board kept on digging the money pit, it is crystal clear that significant liability rests with the RAF and higher committees.

Nimrod MRA4 was closely linked to Sea King ASaC Mk7. During the bidding phase a price reduction was offered if both programmes selected the same radar. (See my earlier comments regarding the political overrule on Sea King that ensured this). This in many ways more complex project was delivered with aplomb. You'd think the Director General would ask the question. Not a chance. Staff who tried to tell him were shut down. Nevertheless, he had been advised: *We've identified a major risk that RMPA shares, and this is what we plan to do.* And then: *We've mitigated the risk, the programme is stable, we recommend RMPA does the same.* Under his direction Nimrod took a different path.

The risk? It was the first identified, and exactly what Mr Hammond admitted 20 years later:

Without stabilising airworthiness, the aircraft can never be certified.

---

57 House of Commons Defence Committee report 'Defence Procurement', 23 July 2003, paragraph 64.

It was a known systemic problem, confirmed in 1992 by the RAF Director of Flight Safety. Two notifications, 17 years apart (and many in between), saying exactly the same thing. Such an unbroken audit trail is what investigators dream of.

Who recommended cancellation? Government will not say. I merely reiterate that the Treasury Solicitor must approve acceptance of equipment off contract when it cannot be certified correctly. But whoever it was acted correctly. Who should have identified this before the contract was awarded? Sorry, wrong question. Who did identify this? MoD's civilian airworthiness specialists, the RAF's Director of Flight Safety, and the RAF's outstanding engineers - in that order. And even British Aerospace themselves. What would have prevented the loss of Nimrod XV230? *Maintaining the build standard*. What would have prevented Nimrod MRA4? *Correct Requirement Scrutiny*. The common denominator is that both processes demand a positive statement that the build standard has been maintained. So why was it policy not to?

A few thoughts on the Nimrod Review

In 2009 Mr Haddon-Cave correctly noted the aircraft Safety Case was invalid. But he blamed the wrong people, entirely avoiding that the Integrated Project Team Leader, a Group Captain, should have *inherited* a valid Safety Case. He didn't. Instead of being criticised he deserved credit for recognising that it had to be resurrected. That it was poorly managed is a separate issue, related to MoD's 'bums on seats' personnel policy and reluctance to fund an activity many still consider a waste of money. The Review would have been better asking why there was no valid Safety Case to begin with. And military aviation better served.

Only Mr Haddon-Cave can say why he dated the failings at 1998, a decade after they actually began; yet accepted and repeated evidence - contained in the same submission - about *savings at the expense of safety*. (His MoD-supplied secretary had been a Nimrod contracts officer in the early 90s and should have declared his knowledge of this). And why did he omit prior written warnings of the precise failings to Ministers (especially Bob Ainsworth and Adam Ingram)?

If you care to read the submissions to him in chronological order, you are left wondering at the integrity of much of the final report. It is one thing to dismiss a submission in its entirety (as Lord Philip did regarding an onboard assassin), but to selectively repeat the key issue (*savings...*), but knowingly misdate it, demands an explanation.

The reason can be found in who he named and praised. One was the Chief of Defence Materiel (Air), an Air Marshal who had reviewed the XV230 Board of Inquiry report. It was not mentioned that in a previous post, as an Air Commodore, he had been MoD(PE)'s Director Maritime in charge of... Nimrod MRA4. And then became Controller Aircraft, responsible for ensuring... airworthiness. That is, he had serious conflicts of interests and should have recused himself. But then one would be left asking why he did not feature in the report - which would have exposed the truth. To protect him it was necessary to deceive.

Also praised was the aforementioned RAF Chief Engineer (1991-96). Normally one might be sympathetic to an Air Chief Marshal in this position, who cannot possibly be expected to have a finger on every detail of his department's work. (Although Haddon-Cave claimed he did). However, the Safety Case is fundamental. If one doesn't exist, or is invalid, then the aircraft cannot fly. In his first three years as Chief Engineer ~28% cuts per annum had been applied to the domain responsible for Safety Cases, with his airworthiness engineers threatened with dismissal for seeking to implement engineering and fiscal policies. Unlike those blamed he did not inherit this situation. He had been a key part of it from the outset.

One must ask, then, why Mr Haddon-Cave complimented these (and other) officers whom he knew had been directly involved. (If minded, one might look at shared Royal Aeronautical Society activities, but others have written of this).[58] The whole truth has not been told. In fact, it has been actively withheld, serving to shelter these individuals. With Philip Hammond's 2014 admission negating most of the Review, the official record consists of two diametrically opposed statements.

An entire reorganisation of MoD was based on this lie. The Military Aviation Authority was formed in 2010, but subsequent accidents and deaths have amply demonstrated it is toothless, and not addressing root causes. A veritable industry of airworthiness consultants has grown from the Review, both in military and civil aviation, when its 587 pages could be condensed into one line: *Do what the mandated regulations tell you to do*.

---

58 'Nimrod - The wrong people blamed' and 'Nimrod - In defence of the Coroner' (James Jones, 2011).

Armoured Cavalry Programme (AJAX)

The Armoured Cavalry Programme, termed AJAX, will deliver a family of six tracked vehicle variants, using a Common Base Platform called ASCOD (Austrian Spanish Cooperation Development). This 1990s design entered service with Austria and Spain in 2002, and the improved v.2 was selected in 2010 for the British Army's Scout Specialist Vehicle. This variant, a little confusingly also called AJAX, is the turreted variant with a 40mm cannon, to be used for Intelligence Surveillance, Target Acquisition and Reconnaissance. Other variants provide vehicle recovery (APOLLO), vehicle repair (ATLAS), an Armoured Personnel Carrier (ARES), Reconnaissance (ARGUS), and Command and Control (ATHENA). AJAX is the most voluminous, with 245 on order, out of a total of 589. The budget is around £5.5Bn.

In April 2021 a further variant was announced - Overwatch - whereby ARES is modified to carry the Brimstone Anti-tank Guided Weapon.

The overall programme is closely related to previously cancelled or 'reset' programmes, such as TRACER (Tactical Reconnaissance Armoured Combat Equipment Requirement), MRAV (Multi-Role Armoured Vehicles), various Warrior Infantry Fighting Vehicle upgrades, Boxer Multi-Role Armoured Vehicle, and FRES (Future Rapid Effects System, also a family of vehicles).

Boxer was a UK/German programme to provide various vehicle variants, but in 2003 MoD withdrew saying it would now deliver the capability under FRES. MoD re-joined the programme in 2018 to provide for its Mechanised Infantry Vehicle. The basic platform can be fitted with 'mission modules' depending on role. But FRES failed calamitously, as did the Warrior programmes. AJAX emerged, and... Sorry. I could go on for another 50 pages and not convey the convoluted history of these vehicle programmes. But, essentially, Boxer and AJAX together cover most of what FRES was supposed to.

The initial requirement was for a Military Off-The-Shelf (MOTS) vehicle, but over 1,200 additional requirements were eventually added; a great many of which were unachievable. When you add any significant change to a MOTS procurement, never mind 1,200, then it is no longer MOTS, it is bespoke with all the attendant risks. 1,200? If the original approval was the answer, it wasn't a good question, and nor was the scrutiny. To reiterate what I said in the previous section, such 'requirement creep' is a common reason for delay.

As ever, MoD and the committees discuss AJAX using the latest 'reset' as the baseline. Observers with a casual interest, who are perhaps aware of these other programmes but not the detail, would assume *they* were delivered successfully 20 years ago, and AJAX replaces *them*. It does not; so while AJAX is officially a few years late, to the Army the capability is decades late.

The AJAX Review

In May 2022 Clive Sheldon QC (now KC) was asked to conduct a review into the programme. His terms of reference were quite narrow, but nevertheless he delivered an excellent 'Lessons Learned Review' in May 2023. He made 24 recommendations, the government accepting 15 and the remainder 'in principle'. *(Are you uncertain, or can you not make your mind up?)* All 24 can be summarised as common sense, already mandated, or existing best practice. The main topics were information flow and technical failings.

The report deals with information comprehensively, accurately conveying the sheer complexity of MoD's organisation, and the number of people who have a finger in the pie but no obvious responsibility or accountability. In short, too many chiefs, not enough Indians. What it does not convey, probably because there was no-one to tell him this, is that the failures he correctly identified had in the past been managed effectively, but successive cut-backs had shut down entire functions. I mentioned this earlier when discussing the Provisioning Authorities. Precisely the same applies, so I won't repeat myself.

Noise

The report dwells at length on the fact AJAX is making trials crews deaf. This was presented by MoD as a revelation, a challenge to be met.

In fact, it's bread and butter stuff, and the noise, vibration, shock, etc. environment in combat vehicles was the subject of Interface Definition Documents (IDD) prepared by the Soldier System Integration Authority (SSIA) in 2002; which AJAX inherited from its predecessor programmes. For example, IDD 075 for FRES, IDD 083 for the Warrior Mid-Life Upgrade, and IDD 077 for the Future Command and Liaison

Vehicle. QinetiQ Systems Integration Department at Farnborough were awarded the contract to manage the process, and the respective Integrated Project Teams provided the necessary information. (Once again raising the question what role the Integration Authority play).

The Defence Committee has held a number of hearings *[sic]* on AJAX, but not once referred to MoD doing this initial work correctly, then allowing it to fall between the cracks. It has cosy chats with a few senior officers, accepting their platitudes, when it should be asking why the IDD work was not continued and 'pulled through'. Liability would become clear, because very few have the authority to waive a critical health and safety *Constraint*. (As distinct from *Limitation*, which can be worked around).

It was only in 2011 that MoD responded to QinetiQ's persistence, who unsurprisingly proposed implementing the mandated protocols that had been developed over the past two decades. Astonishingly they were snubbed, and nothing was done.

On 16 December 2021 it was announced to Parliament:

> *'A report from the Defence Safety Authority in May 2020 identifying some of these issues and entitled "Serious Safety Concerns on Ajax" was retracted and not pursued, either by the DSA or by the project team in Defence Equipment and Support. Multiple warnings from the Dstl and from the Armoured Trials and Development Unit, which was running the trials, were not actioned, even when the ATDU commanding officer questioned the approach as having the potential to expose soldiers to a known hazard, which he stated was not a defendable position'.*

Only now were QinetiQ engaged, and matters have since improved. So many years, so much money wasted, and so many soldiers disabled.

Mr Sheldon reported that a 3-Star Review had been held on 13 November 2020:

> *'The issue was discussed as a "headset" problem, rather than a major engineering issue or programmatic risk, and it was reported that GDLS-UK did not agree that there was any noise or vibration problem with the vehicles. The issue of headsets and their interaction with vehicles concerning noise was highly contentious and a matter of dispute with GDLS-UK. Headsets were Government Furnished Equipment, i.e. supplied by MoD not (the AJAX prime contractor), although the company was responsible for integrating them with*

the vehicles' communication systems'.[59]

We've been here before...

The AJAX contract with General Dynamics (GD) requires the company to integrate the legacy Racal RA195 Combat Mk2 headset. But it emerged GD did not use the Mk2 when conducting testing and trials. This reveals a number of failures, none mentioned in the report:

- The Mk2 provides both passive and active attenuation (the earshells and Active Noise Reduction, respectively). The Racal website simply says the former attenuates high frequencies, the latter low. This is largely meaningless. Under the Control of Noise at Work Regulations 2005, the Lower Exposure Action Value for noise at the ear of a user is 80dB(A) and the Upper Exposure Action Value 85dB(A). Digital ANR was developed when it was believed the former was to be 75dB(A), and in August 1999 achieved 73dB(A). (The legislation was delayed and it was decided to proceed at risk). Its predecessor, Analog ANR, was developed against the 85dB(A) figure, and achieved 83dB(A). (The lower the figure, the better. A 3dB reduction halves the sound energy). The main advance on DANR was its programmable nature.

- The key issue is functional safety, whereby one addresses the standing risk of an equipment being safe in one application, but not in another. It would seem MoD simply assumed the Mk2 would be fine in AJAX (knowing it was already inadequate in Warrior); when any noise reduction system must address the noise dose in individual environments. That is, one carries out a noise survey in each platform to ascertain the damaging and annoying noises, and tailors the design accordingly (e.g. via software).

- The Army's design philosophy is that the headset is part of the vehicle, not Personal Protective Equipment. Once again, MoD has failed to learn from previous programmes, where it was emphasised that the system must be individually fitted and issued as personal kit.

- The report confirms that, eventually, the AJAX project office in Defence Equipment & Support (DE&S) agreed that GD instrument the trials vehicles.[60] This was clearly presented to Mr Sheldon as a piece of innovative thinking, omitting that it is the first task in any

59 Armoured Cavalry Programme (AJAX) Lesson Learned Review, paragraph 6.6.1.1.
60 Armoured Cavalry Programme (AJAX) Lesson Learned Review, paragraph 7.4.13.

hearing protection programme, and had been rejected in 2011. This is so fundamental, I believe it incumbent upon Mr Sheldon to revise and reissue his report.

But the two biggest failures at a corporate level are this:

1. An Ajax Noise and Vibration Review was commissioned by the Permanent Under Secretary (PUS), conducted by an internal team between 21 June and 14 July 2021, led by MoD's Director of Health, Safety and Environmental Protection (HS&EP). At Finding 2, he said: *'Programme staff in DE&S and Army did not have the necessary experience and knowledge to deeply understand the management of noise and vibration'*. Given the aforementioned ANR programmes, and the direct follow-on work of the Soldier System Integration Authority, this is simply wrong. MoD <u>does</u> have the experience and knowledge, and actually owns the IPR to the world's leading ANR system.

2. On 25 August 1998 the Directorate of Operational Requirements (Sea) sought advice from the ANR/DANR programme manager on establishing a Hearing Protection Integrated Project Team.[61] He replied with a draft Board Submission (Business Case).[62] Plainly, no progress was made; but should not detract from (1) above.

Finally, Mr Sheldon recommended that key staff remain in post longer. This sounds easy, but in practice is difficult. First, there is the anti-corruption policy I mentioned earlier. But more fundamentally there is the natural desire of the individual to advance. MoD used to permit in-post ('merit') promotion, but it was not substantive. To move away, one had to revert to one's substantive grade. In my experience, this only tended to work at the end of one's career, and in cases where (e.g.) family considerations took primacy. Nevertheless, the point was well made.

In summary? The Defence Lines of Development broke down. There was no oversight by the appointed oversight body. The level of incompetence was truly colossal.

---

61 Letter DOR(Sea)G/626/9/3, 25 August 1998.
62 Letter D/DHP/24/4/93/43, 1 September 1998.

The Big Wheel

The waste I have described was predicted and notified, yet nothing was done. Where were the independent regulators? There weren't any. The wastrels were allowed to self-regulate, stifling debate. The ability to meet time, cost and performance criteria became irrelevant.

Those who seek to do their job properly can seldom operate successfully within MoD's version of bureaucracy. They need an adhocracy; a flexible, adaptable and more informal organisation encouraging free-thinking. I have offered many examples of failing projects being resurrected, problems solved, and waste avoided, by ignoring the bureaucracy and creating an adhocracy.

But it is not enough to know what actions led to success, and by whom. It must be known who stood against them and tried to prevent that success, and what their motivations were. And why they continue to succeed. The classic example I offered was in the section 'The needs of the many'. There is nothing in the teachings of the MoD bureaucracy that prepares you for the Service knowingly providing ~2% of the necessary funding, and then complaining about slow progress. As I proposed earlier, all MoD staff should be given this as a case study to solve. It reveals <u>everything</u> that is wrong with Defence <u>Acquisition</u>. Crack it, and you've cracked it!

The policies I have discussed, in particular *savings at the expense of safety*, have cast a lingering pall over equipment acquisition, and aviation safety in particular. The financial waste remains astronomical. But far more important is the waste of life, and the refusal to prevent recurrence. I submit to you that the totality of the evidence, and the unbroken 35-year audit trail I have set out, validates the book title. MoD is indeed the Citadel of Waste. But not all of it. Not by any means, and I hope I have made clear that it retains many excellent staff who strive daily against all the odds to deliver what the Services need.

ANNEX - Defence Lines of Development definitions

Concepts & Doctrine

The intellectual underpinning for capabilities and operational processes that are likely to be used to accomplish an activity in the future. Doctrine represents the enduring principles that guide military forces in their actions, as well as a codification of existing best practice. It is authoritative, but requires judgment in application.

Organisation

The operational and non-operational organisational relationships of people. It typically includes military force structures, MoD civilian organisational structures, and Defence contractors providing support.

Personnel

The timely provision of sufficient, capable and motivated personnel to deliver Defence outputs, both now and in the future.

Infrastructure

The acquisition, development, management and disposal of all fixed, permanent buildings and structures, land, utilities and facility management services (both Hard & Soft Facility Management) in support of Defence capabilities. It includes estate development and structures that support military and civilian personnel.

Information

The coherent identification of data, information and knowledge requirements for capabilities and all processes designed to gather, handle data and exploit information and knowledge. Data is defined as raw facts, without inherent meaning, used by humans and systems. Information is defined as 'data placed in context'. Knowledge is Information applied to a particular situation.

Training

The provision of the means to practise, develop and validate, within constraints, the practical application of a common military doctrine to deliver a military capability.

Equipment

The provision of military platforms, systems and weapons, expendable and non-expendable (including updates to legacy systems), needed to outfit/equip an individual, group or organisation.

Logistics

The means of planning and executing the operational movement and maintenance of forces. In its most comprehensive sense, it relates to those aspects of military operations which deal with: the design and development, acquisition, storage, transport, distribution, maintenance, evacuation, disposition of materiel; the transport of personnel; the acquisition, construction, maintenance, operation, and disposal of facilities; the acquisition or furnishing of services, medical and health-service support.

In addition to the eight DLODs, and notwithstanding the general practice of denying funding for Interoperability, the DLOD policy (correctly) includes it as an overarching factor that must be considered when any DLOD is being addressed. It is defined as:

The ability of UK Forces and, when appropriate, forces of partner and other nations to train, exercise and operate effectively together in the execution of assigned missions and tasks. In the context of DLOD, Interoperability also covers interaction between single Services, UK Defence capabilities, Other Government Departments and the civil aspects of interoperability, including compatibility with Civil Regulations. Interoperability is used in the literal sense and is not a compromise lying somewhere between integration and deconfliction.

Terms and abbreviations

AML	Air Member Logistics
AMSO	Air Member Supply and Organisation (RAF)
ANR	Active Noise Reduction
AOC	Air Officer Commanding
ARI	Airborne Radio Installation
ARP	Applied Research Package
BER	Beyond Economic Repair
CAMO	Continuing Airworthiness Maintenance Organisation
CDP	Chief of Defence Procurement
CEO	Chief Executive Officer
CHART	Chinook Airworthiness Review Team (and its report)
DCC	Dismounted Close Combat
DE&S	Defence Equipment & Support
DEC	Directorate of Equipment Capability
DERA	Defence Evaluation and Research Agency
DF	Direction Finding
DGAS2	Director General Air Systems 2 (later Executive Director 1 of the Defence Procurement Agency)
DGSM	Director General Support Management (RAF)
DIA	Director Internal Audit
DLOD	Defence Lines of Development
DPA	Defence Procurement Agency
DRA	Defence Research Agency
DSAC	Defence Scientific Advisory Council
ELINT	Electronic Intelligence
ETC	Environmental Test Chamber
FAA	Federal Aviation Administration
FIST	Future Integrated Soldier Technology
FOAEW	Future Organic Airborne Early Warning

FONA	Flag Officer Naval Aviation
FTS	Flying Training School
GFX	Government Furnished Equipment, Facilities, Information and Services
IAC	Investment Approvals Committee
IDD	Interface Definition Document
IFF	Identification, Friend or Foe
IPC	Illustrated Parts Catalogue
IPT	Integrated Project Team
ITT	Invitation to Tender
LERC	Local Equipment Repair Committee
LPO	Local Purchase Order
MAA	Military Aviation Authority
MADGE	Microwave Aircraft Digital Guidance Equipment
MASC	Maritime Airborne Surveillance and Control
MCP	(Directorate of) Military Communications Projects
MDDLS	Microwave Dummy Deck Landing System
MFTS	Military Flying Training System
MoD	Ministry of Defence
MoD(PE)	Ministry of Defence (Procurement Executive)
MRA	Maritime Reconnaissance Attack
NARO	Naval Aircraft Repair Organisation
PDS	Post Design Services
PFI	Private Finance Initiative
PUS	Permanent Under Secretary of State for Defence
QFI	Qualified Flying Instructor
RMPA	Replacement Maritime Patrol Aircraft
SAL	Slingsby Aviation Limited
SRO	Senior Responsible Owner
VGS	Volunteer Gliding Squadron

Printed in Great Britain
by Amazon

36290401R00108